Heart Sick.

Book Therapy for the Discouraged

Connecting the dots between hope, disappointment, and healing.

Conscious Coore

Table of Contents

Hope Deferred

What is hope?

Is it the belief that good things will always happen? Is it the belief that all of the essential things in life are guaranteed?

Are all things we hope for truly good and beneficial in nature?

Is everything that we lose a necessary loss for some sort of greater cause?

Maybe that's the real question right there... is loss *necessary*? It seems to be easier to handle loss of money, jobs, relationships and such if we can look back and attribute the loss to some sort of subsequent good. It feels worth it if we can reflect on it and say, "I wouldn't be where I am today if I hadn't let that go".

As we approach the topic of hope, we must do so soberly. It's okay to not be sure, but there is one thing of which we must be certain, and that is this: we don't have all the answers. Our understanding of hope and faith is evolving even when we are inactive in our pursuits of it. On the other side of this, hope and faith evolves more rapidly when we are in rapid pursuit of it. When we are courageous and curious enough to analyze hope – and brave enough to exercise hope – perspective changes. When perspective changes, unimaginable things happen.

Sometimes, sick people are healed – and granted, sometimes they are not. Sometimes, loved ones live years beyond a bad prognosis – but, of course, sometimes they don't. Sometimes, you get the dream job – and sometimes, you are overlooked.

We may hope for the success of a relationship not knowing that it would turn toxic. We may hope for a position on a job not knowing that it would eventually call for a breach of personal morals. We may hope for health and long life for close family and friends, not knowing that aggressive illness is on the horizon.

When we look on the bright side of hope, we can say that if you don't have hope, you cannot possibly expect to have good things. Without hope, you are less likely to create and pursue opportunities that have the potential to improve and transform your life. But when we look at all sides of hope, it doesn't seem as promising. It appears as though just because I have hope doesn't mean I have a guaranteed positive outcome. It would also seem that if I dare to hope for anything too specific, I might be setting myself up for some sort of disappointment in the end.

Disappointment is a part of life, but frequent encounters with disappointment may be where the hope that is within us takes its most brutal beating. There are seasons where it is as if every time you step out to hope for something great and life changing, something else arises which impacts your time, resources, and opportunity to see it manifest. While noticing this pattern of disappointment, it might almost seem safer, *smarter even* to retire the language of hope to brace yourself for bad news.

At times, I have both felt and said *if I expect nothing, I can't be disappointed.* I would lean on the evidence of my past to justify negative assumptions about my desires, my future, and other people as well. Though I still inform my decisions with the evidence of my past, my perspective on faith and disappointment has changed. So, I have my speculations about hope that I would like to share as we start the conversation about the sick heart.

These are not definite answers, they are just speculations.

Hope is a belief for something that is personally considered a favorable outcome.
Hope is not the belief that good things will always happen as much as it is a fair enough belief that a good thing *can* happen given a scenario.

Hope is believing that everything that is essential to life and wellness can be found if it is sought out and waited for patiently.

I suspect that not everything we hope for is truly good, but we often don't notice the hidden variables that lie in wait which would negatively impact the objects we hope for.

Not *everything* that is loss is necessary for what may be considered a greater good. Perhaps you can find occasion where a relationship was better off ended, or where loss of material things helped to alleviate financial burden. However, on the other hand, our schools, communities, and churches have seen and suffered many losses that were of benefit to no one. We have seen loss due to human error, not divine intervention, and the nation is impacted by these losses every day.

But who is to say that a loss was necessary or unnecessary? In the grand scheme of things, our human insight and foresight can be quite limited. Being that we cannot truly know every detail of our own lives, it is impossible to understand the meaning and the reason behind everything we experience as it is being experienced. Loss creates complicated and complex perspectives on reality and at the end of the day, the best way to know why we suffer the things that we suffer, is to have a healthy perspective on the loss. A healthy perspective is had on the other side of healing, and even then, we may never know fully why things unfold the way they do.

I think of my own father.

For reasons that are irrelevant now, there was a long stretch of time where I had not spoken to my father. There had always been some brokenness in our relationship since about 6th grade, but every desire I had to make us whole and functional came to a stark end after a conversation that we had only a few months before my wedding.

Up to that point, visits and phone calls were consistently strained and volatile. As a child, he would lecture for hours talking in riddles that I didn't understand, but I loved him so much that I allowed my mental capacity to be stretched until I could connect the dots between everything he said. Frequently, wars between my mother and father would become battles between him and I but between the headaches, tears, and late nights, I still wanted my dad. I wanted his friendship so badly that I strove to understand and to prove to him that I understood. For as long as I could remember, I participated in conversations with him that were far beyond my years because I felt that if he saw that I was the only one listening, it would earn his love, his trust and some sort of stability in our relationship. As I got older, things only got worse, and often times it felt like even though he wasn't my enemy, I was his.

We can all be found broken somewhere within, so to this day I don't hold anything against him. I do recognize though that much of my childhood with him was made up of me fighting to remain a "daddy's girl" and allowing the shards of his brokenness to penetrate me mentally and emotionally. Loving a broken person is going to be tough for anyone, especially when you are a child.

In that season of silence between us, I had fasted and prayed for him, but I had also decided to start a new chapter of life that didn't include me being at the mercy of his brokenness. Happily, I would soon find out that while I was continuing to become a woman, he was also becoming the type of person who I had always longed for him to be. The first conversation I had with him after the stretch of silence was a breath of fresh air. As I listened to him talk, I heard grace, joy and peace vibrate through his voice, which was good to hear.

But what moved me wasn't that first phone call.

It was the several phone calls afterward which were consistently the same. I continued to see this man that I had longed for him to be for over ten years. For the first time in my mature years, we genuinely connected emotionally and spiritually. I was no longer striving to understand someone who could not be understood. It was as if he wasn't afraid to love me anymore. I still felt a slight panic when his name would flash across my phone as an incoming call, but I had even more moments of relief and euphoria when his words toward me were funny, loving, enlightening, and pure. I had my dad back, and I was figuring out ways to get used to it. Eventually, I couldn't wait to talk to him to share what was new in my life and my marriage. He was one of the first to find out when I became pregnant.

I saw the purest joy in him when he found out that I would have a child. My father had six biological children – five girls and one boy. I will never forget how he accurately and joyfully guessed that I would have a boy and I was looking forward to the birth of my son as something to experience with my father.

I had about eleven years with a man who was strong, mobile, present, and loving. I spent the next twelve years with a man who was hurt, afraid, wounded and discouraged. I had two years with a man who was caring, patient, understanding, and full of joy, and all of them were my father. Yet, I had only about a month to imagine him as a man that my child would soon meet.

Just like that, he had passed away.

I cannot tell you it was necessary for me to lose my father months before his grandson, my firstborn, could meet him. I don't think it was necessary, but I don't know. What I can tell you is that I hoped my son could meet this version of his grandfather and not the one I grew up fighting to love.

What I can tell you is that after his passing, I discovered myself in a new way and found fragments of my experiences with my father influencing my current conditions. I didn't just grieve over his death. I grieved over the trauma that I sustained while he was alive. I grieved over the fact that he did not live long enough to overhaul or replace the negative memories I had of him. Even though the last two years of his life had been so full of love and light, it did not erase the fact that when I desperately needed him to be that, I couldn't find him. He was alive, but not well, which was almost the same as him not being around at all.

While my reality extends far beyond the loss of my father, the way that I relate to the loss itself has impacted me and has further potential to impact everything that makes up my reality; from marriage, to parenting, to my very identity which was molded by his presence, his absence *and* his death.

It was not wrong for me to hope. It wasn't wrong for me to suffer loss. It wasn't wrong for me to grieve. All of these things are a part of life.

I asked myself, if occasional disappointment is guaranteed, then what is the point of faith? If faith is the substance of things hoped for and the evidence of things not seen, then it would seem appropriate to hope for the impossible and envision the unforeseeable. You can probably name a few things that you have hoped for and at the time thought *all I need is a little faith and God will make it happen,* yet here we are and perhaps it still has not come to pass.

I believe in the power of resurrection, but death is designed by God to be irreversible, unless He chooses to reverse the irreversible – which we would call a miracle. Even if we hope for the dead to be raised, it may not necessarily happen. *But didn't Jesus raise the dead?* Eventually, it begins to feel like we've all been lied to about who God is and what it takes to get Him to move for one like He's done for others. It can make faith seem like a huge superstitious gamble to people who are neither gamblers nor superstitious. We have raised questions about hope, but now it seems important to ask the question: *What is faith?*

My speculation is that faith is the element of belief that helps us to have focus, hone vision and even recover from loss and disappointment as it is rooted in our knowledge of who God is and what *He* desires. Faith needs hope in order to manifest the promises of God but *hope* needs faith in order to be grounded in what is true, what is pure, what is holy and what is purposeful. Hope and faith work together.

So, though we may hope for the dead to be raised again, only God knows the highest truth about what happens within the timing of a life and when that life is to come to an end. I think about how Jesus' entire purpose was to die. Though He lived for a while, it was His death that the Lord was ultimately building toward. Because of His death, we now see that death has just as much purpose as life and as resurrection. However, only He knows when any of those outcomes will truly lead to something pure, and holy according to His purpose. So, I guess that would also raise a few even more important questions:

- What is your hope based on?
- What is your faith in?
- Who (on Earth or in Heaven) do you trust most?

A lot of the things we hope for are based on or birthed from needs. In order to live, your mother has to carry, deliver, and nurture you into higher levels of independence. This bears hope that you were not only born, but *desired*, loved, and cared for.

In order to survive childhood, you must have guardians or a family to provide sustenance, shelter, and direction. This bears the hope that family can be both near and present to provide the intimacy and support that you need so long as you are dependent on them.

After entering adulthood, you want to be able to sustain life independently, so you pursue some form of work or purpose. Again, this bears a hope for clarity and success with schooling, jobs, and other lucrative endeavors.

We don't all hope for the same exact things, but we do all have expectations that live within three domains: Family, Relationships, and Work/Purpose and within these aspects of life do we often experience the most loss and the most sorrow.

Already, you can probably think of a handful or more encounters where what you hoped for, or needed, simply did not exist in the way that you needed it to. It is incredibly easy to have a heap of disappointments well before we have even discovered the depths of our own personalities. In some cases, this heap of disappointment progresses from just disappointment, to a constant, walking state of grief.

For the purpose of this book, I don't limit the meaning of grief to the death of a loved one, though grief is often experienced in that context. Furthermore, grief and disappointment are not the only reasons that many people have what I refer to in this book as the sick heart. Grief, by its simplest definition, is the complex response to loss. We have all been disappointed at some point in our lives, no matter how deep we bury the pain. Throughout this book, we will be exploring the overlooked and minimized losses that occur in a lifetime and its impact on everyday living.

If you are reading this book, you are in for a look at how hope and disappointment fit into big picture of faith. It is with the hope that each of you can see yourself in the journey of finding healing after abandonment, discouragement, heartbreak, and devastating disappointment. Not every disappointment turns into grief and not all grief is linked to childhood trauma, but I have found that adulthood experiences are often connected to traumatic experiences that happened in earlier years, especially in childhood. Because of that, seemingly minor setbacks and frustrations catapult people into aggressive and elongated seasons of grief and hopelessness. It can be difficult to find healing and hope again without tending to old wounds as if they mean something – because they *do.*

As you read, it's important to know that the journey that I hope to take you on will require three things (outside of the book itself) endurance, a journal and Jesus. In addition to that, you may also find that what is right for you is in fact getting support from a mental health professional. This book is intended to serve as a form of counsel and a source for healing, but not expected to substitute for the service of faithful, trained and caring counselors or therapists.

Curing the sick heart brought on by loss and disappointment requires acknowledging our experiences and examining our hopes and expectations. When we get to a place where we can accurately analyze our faith in Jesus, truthfully recount experiences, and honestly acknowledge hopes, we can begin connecting dots.

In this book, I am calling that heart sickness many things: *sadness, hopelessness, confusion, anger, resentment, disappointment, fear, anxiety, depression, grief* -- the list goes on. To the person reading this book, you are not alone. This sickness is an unknown epidemic. In the same ink that I write this, I do also say Jesus is a healer -- but first, we have to unpack.

hope deferred makes the heart sick, but when the desire comes it is a tree of life.

proverbs 13:12 kjv

unrelenting disappointment leaves the heartsick, but a sudden good break can turn life around.

proverbs 13:12 msg

Journal Entry:

Think about what you hope for or have previously hoped for in your family, relationships, career, and success.

What, if anything, has changed about those hopes and why?

Heart Sick

Everything that you may have journaled, discussed and uncovered about your life outside of this book is what we will refer to as *your truth*. There is no part of your story that will need to be hidden or revised, but what will hopefully change, in a positive way, is your perspective on your story. In order for that to happen, there should be a readiness to grow in your belief in the scriptures.

It can be uncomfortable to view the Bible as truth when there are so many cryptic things within it. Nonetheless, it is in the scriptures that we read about the sick heart and it is from the scriptures that we will take away the truth about its healing.

With that being said, let's visit a well-loved saying:
Follow your heart ... that's the one.

When we encourage ourselves and each other to follow the heart, what is it that we are implying should take a lead in our lives? When we speak of the symbolic heart, we are referencing the dimension of self that is informed by our perspectives and our experiences. Those perspectives and experiences all combine to fuel intense emotions like passion, love, and desire – all of which we recognize as *matters* of the heart.

Mainstream media will say that the key to a happy life is to follow your heart, but scripture suggests that our hearts do not always lead us to a fairytale life as we might imagine. When I look at the wealth of wisdom in the Word of God two main ideas about the heart stand out to me concerning its sickness.

1. The heart of man is wicked and the only One who can know it fully and thoroughly is God. (Jeremiah 17:9)
2. The heart must be watched over with fidelity, because whatever is in it influences and creates the issues of life (Proverbs 4:23)

One other instance where a heart is referred to as 'sick' is in Ezekiel 16:30, when God reveals Jerusalem's lust for idols as an issue of their *sick heart.*

Does this mean that everything we desire is evil? Of course not.

What this shows us, more than anything, is that we are born with hearts that are prone to sickness. Before the heart was ever sick, it was wicked. That wickedness speaks to the primitive human condition and is the exact reason why we needed the sacrifice of Christ and the Spirit of God unto life. From the day we are born, the human heart is in need of a guardian – adult leaders who create an environment full of truth and safety. Consequently, in the absence of truth and safety, children can experience a broken heart at a very early age. The fragments of that broken heart can remain for years until it can finally be healed in environments that are full of what was once in deficit: truth and safety.

Whenever we make mention of a broken heart, we are describing an experience where a thing that we once held closely in passionate love stopped functioning to serve a need and thereby caused great pain. Studies show that in moments and seasons of intense disappointment, what we call a broken heart in a metaphorical sense can be felt physically as something very similar to a heart attack, including chest pain and shortness of breath. This phenomenon, known as *broken heart syndrome,* involves

irregularity in the hearts normal pumping – while the other parts of the heart function normally or with more force.

The physical heart is responsible for pumping blood throughout the body to supply it with nutrients and oxygen and get rid of harmful wastes. The phenomenon of *broken heart syndrome* is evidence of how issues of the figurative heart can be mirrored in the physical body and if the heart is not transformed and healed, it can lead us to great depths of darkness, heaviness, and physical pain. The figurative heart is therefore as vital to the spirit man as the heart organ is to the physical body and should be examined with great caution.

For the sake of truth and healing, we will constantly have to subject our perspectives and our experiences to the truth of the Word of God if we desire to see healing from the times that we were left abandoned while following an untransformed heart. If we can acknowledge the flawed condition of our hearts, our minds can be opened to rather follow the Spirit of God to the point where the passions and desires of our hearts are purified.

If you wanted to examine your heart, you might ask yourself a few questions:

What do I genuinely hope for?
Why do I want what I hope for?
Why do I feel like I am so deserving of this?
Are my hopes truly leading me to what I want long-term? Do my hopes align with the Will of the Father for my life? Am I willing to submit my desires to The Lord in exchange for His best?

When I think about the answers to these questions for myself, it helps me sort through how and why I gravitate to certain passions. Sometimes a deep enough reflection
might even lessen my yearning for whatever I intensely desire. That doesn't necessarily mean that my desires are wrong, or instantly change. It just helps to lessen the pitfalls of idealism and false hope which can only make living in faith *with* disappointment more complicated.

Before any healing can take place, we have to be prepared to look at our hearts with clear and balanced perspective. Rather than being trusted, we ought to examine it (1 Cor 11:28), guard it, and ultimately allow God to change it as we take rest and delight in being with Him (Psalm 37:4). Though nothing can separate us from the love of God, a sick heart can indeed lead us to make choices that separate us from the will of God and leave us desperate for something more.

The Epidemic

I find it amazing that I am the only human being who has lived my life and who sees everything *exactly* the way I see it. No one else in the entire world knows every single detail of my life except me and there is no other human being that could have lived in the house that I grew up in and come out with the exact same experience or memories that I left that house with.

There is something very intimate, unique and fascinating about perspective. Our sweetest most intimate relationships are had with people who are neither too busy nor too afraid to get close and share a lens with us. We have to cherish people who step outside of their own experience just to visualize the experience of someone else. The truth is, though, that many of us are reluctant to share our perspectives on our experience with someone else for a number of reasons.

> *It's too complicated*
> *It's not that serious.*
> *Very few will understand.*
> *I don't want to burden anybody.*
> *It's embarrassing.*
> *It's hopeless and there's nothing they can do about it*
> *anyway.*

Some of the reasons I give to stay locked in my head and away from the world feel very legitimate to me unless I encounter someone who can handle and understand my perspective. The interesting thing about perspective is that it doesn't change the experience. It just changes the way we see it. Healing comes when we can look at our experience through a lens of faith, separating our past from our future and allowing the One we believe in to drive what we hope for. It's easier said than done though because… "feelings".

When we look through the lens of faith, the first rule is that we do not base our beliefs on our feelings. Contrary to popular belief though, feelings do matter and they are essential in matters of mental health and the broken heart. Fact: when it comes to a matter of obedience to God, how you feel about your assignment or instructions do not waive your responsibility to do what the Lord says to do. However, it is critically important to be mindful of *what* your feelings are in every circumstance because those feelings reveal an area where God's truth needs to encounter *your truth*.

Take a heart attack, for example. When the body is suffering a heart attack, there are feelings associated with it to signal that something is wrong with this major organ. The victim of the heart attack will feel tightness and pain in the chest or arms, as well as the jaw, back or neck, but the *feelings* don't stop there. The person suffering the heart attack may feel the clammy chill of a cold sweat along with difficulty breathing and dizziness. When all of these symptoms converge, we instantly are aware that the person is sick and that something is wrong with the heart.

Right away, anyone in the room would call for an ambulance seeking the help from doctors. We want someone who will listen to the symptoms and ask follow-up questions. We want a caring professional that will take a look through a lens or an X-Ray to see what they can detect to find the source of the heart attack and provide direction for what to do next. Whether it's surgery, a changed diet, or a more active lifestyle we hardly care, we just want answers. We want instructions. We want someone to help deal with the root issue that caused the feelings.

Imagine, now, if we take this scenario and equate the seriousness of it to other issues of the heart and mind. Mental, emotional, and spiritual issues are just as capable of producing physiological symptoms. Just as sure as there can be physical trauma to the brain or heart, intangible and invisible trauma can be done to the spirit of the mind and the figurative heart.

Most people do not take sickness in the mind as seriously as sickness in the body and even fewer people are aware that there can be sickness in the heart. We will rarely urge professional care for such issues. We rarely rush to seek help from the nearest doctor. We hardly will run a quick search on the internet to diagnose the situation and look into what would be the best next steps. However, heart sickness is just as much an epidemic as heart disease and it's time to tend to heart issues much more than we tend to do as a world and as victims.

Trauma in the Truth

Curing the sick heart brought on by disappointment requires acknowledging our experiences and examining our hopes and expectations.

One of the reasons why it can be difficult to normalize proactive mental wellness is because of the stigma associated with mental illness. Additionally, there is a presumption that the only people who need such support are those who have been exposed to violent, unusual and extreme environments. While everyone's experience may not have been violent, unusual or extreme, I would push every reader to think beyond these realms and look at other unconventionally traumatic events that people experience from day to day.

By definition, any event *can* qualify as being traumatic if it was extremely distressing and created damage or injury to the psyche. With this being the case, what is traumatic for one person may not be nearly as distressing to the next individual but is equally as important to address and receive healing regarding. However, before any of us arrive at the place of healing, we have to be prepared to see our experiences for what they are. Within this book is a safe space to do so.

Know your truth. Speak your truth. *Your truth* is whatever is known and experienced by the person who is speaking. What you consider to be true, whether or not it is debatable, is essential to know and be fully aware of. If a person cannot face the truth of what they believe about family, God, opportunity, purpose, etc. the basis for coming out of confusion into clarity is unrealistic and nearly impossible. The reason it is nearly impossible is because if you should encounter a Biblical truth that has the power to heal your perspective, it instantly comes in violent contact with what is previously rooted in your mind as the truth.

There is no exception to this rule until you become willing to reexamine what you call truth. Your thought life is born and cultivated out of what you believe to be true. This is why seeking some form of counseling or therapy can be the best route for many who are seeking healing. Taking these routes of healing help to deconstruct some of the untrue or outright toxic beliefs that we may have about ourselves, others, and the world around us. The role of a therapist or counselor is to dig beneath the surface to uncover the foundations of the many hidden beliefs held and then trace it back to manifested thoughts and behaviors.

Digging is a major aspect of healing. Digging is the process of seeking more depth into the dirt... that is, the dirt of our own lives! We all have dirt. For some of us, it is easy to be honest with self, while for others it may be the hardest thing, but learning or confronting the truth can reveal a lot about how we become so heart sick to begin with. With that being said, it is gravely important to take on full responsibility of facing the truth of your experience through your own lens.
Is it all going to be perceived as, right? *Maybe, but not always.*

Is it going to sound a little dysfunctional? *Hopefully at least a little.*
If nothing about your life and your story sounds a little dysfunctional, you may not be telling the whole truth. We all have baggage. There's nothing to hide, and there is plenty to unpack.

The wonderful and necessary thing about laying out the truth, even the smallest details, is that it helps us to acknowledge the trauma that we do in fact sustain throughout our living. In this age of technology, we have a reputation for moving too quickly and wanting instant results. Yet, I am in belief that any person from any generation can be found guilty of simply moving too fast to *feel.* We don't have time to feel the impact of our experiences and rarely understand the need to acknowledge what is happening in the mind. As a result, strongholds form and start to protect toxic thoughts hidden in the spirit of the mind (Ephesians 4:23). In the chapter on healing, we will discuss how to get rid of strongholds, but for now it's important to spend some time acknowledging feelings.

Imagine if you could be in need of medical attention but had no alert of the injury through pain or discomfort. What if we had no senses to know when we were being burned? Certainly, we would expose those wounds and injuries to environments that could worsen our own condition. Furthermore, if we have no time or ability to stop and feel what is happening to us physically, then we stand the chance of sustaining injury after injury.

In the same way, if we have no time or ability to stop and feel what is happening to us mentally, emotionally, and spiritually, then we stand the chance of sustaining injury to ourselves in multiple unseen dimensions. Before we know it, we are walking and functioning with the injury but worsening in our state of mind and state of being.

How we think about trauma can be part of the reason why so many of us do not treat our own with intention and care.

Research shows that a potentially traumatic event is more prone to leave an individual with longer-lasting emotional and psychological trauma if:

- *The individual was unprepared for the event*
- *The event occurred out of the blue*
- *The person felt powerless to prevent the event*
- *The event occurred repeatedly (such as child abuse)*
- *If the event involved extreme cruelty*
- *If the event occurred during the childhood years*[1]

Do you see your own experiences in any parts of the list above?

Be willing to discover potential trauma within your own experiences without comparing it to someone else's suffering. You have to know or at least be willing to discover where and when you became broken even if you do not discover it all. Often times, the parts of our experience wherein much of the trauma takes place is in childhood, capitalized upon in preadolescence and then fully manifested in adult relationships and endeavors. Nonetheless, when there is injury at any level of consciousness, there are always signs that indicate that healing is necessary. It's not enough to medicate the symptoms. True healing involves getting to the root cause of the pain.

This part of tending to the sick heart is probably the most challenging because it requires intrinsic motivation and accountability to self. In order to search your past,

even your childhood, to recover your experiences, both good and bad, you have to build a level of dedication to yourself. It is not enough to face your truth for others' sake. In order to endure, you have to face the truth of every experience, every expectation, every disappointment, and every failure for yourself.

Sorting out whether anything of the past was right or wrong should not be done prematurely because it will distract your digging. The past is complicated and while some of it is most certainly wrong, and some of it is absolutely right, what many people find trouble doing is admitting that *it* happened, and *it* made me feel a certain way, and I never really knew how to deal with *it*, so I never did.

1 (Cascade Behavioral Health Hospital, 2019)

Journal Entry:

What are some experiences in your life that you can identify as being distressing or potentially traumatic?

How have these experiences impacted your life?

Grief

Have you ever misplaced a $20 bill?

I could be wrong, but I don't think it matters how much money you have in the bank account. When you place a fully intact crispy (or dingy) green twenty-dollar bill in your wallet or pocket, it creates a small sense of financial security. This sense of security is so strong that there is an entire population of people who would agree that a little piece of them dies when they have to use it to purchase a small, relatively useless item only to receive ones, fives and change in return. That twenty-dollar bill in your pocket represents possibility.

Granted, I live in New York City and there is not too much that $20 can buy even for a week's worth of grocery from the store around the block, but that does not change the feeling that I get if I were to find one in a pair of jeans while sorting the laundry. Nor does it change how I would feel if I thought I was walking around with twenty dollars' worth of security and then found out it was missing.

My process when I lose something, whether it is money, a debit card, my license, keys, or whatever, is that I first retrace my steps. I can't bring myself to focus on anything else until I have spent a great deal of time looking for whatever that object is or at least until I am sure that I know where to look if I should need it. It starts out as a small sense of panic but a healthy amount of hope that if I just stay calm, retrace my steps and look for it, I will find it.

For the first thirty minutes of looking for the lost item, I am holding onto, but admittedly losing hope as time progresses. So, I take a break and consider that maybe I am missing something. At this point, I am probably also praying very seriously that the Holy Spirit leads me "into all truth" about where I misplaced the item and whether it was stolen. Frankly, once I am at the point of trying to figure out who stole from me, I am very close to peak frustration.

Sometimes, after I have done all I could, something clicks, a memory rings, or the Holy Spirit speaks and I know where to go to find the thing I have been looking for. Other times, I have to wait a few hours or days to realize that I needed to look in an altogether different place. Naturally, though, there have been more than a few times that I just never found what I was looking for. At that point, it sets in that what I hoped for is out of reach and I can hardly find anyone to blame – except maybe myself.

Now, I don't want to minimize severe mental struggle to something as small as losing money that will be replaced at the next paycheck. At the same time, for someone who is down to their last twenty- dollar bill, this scenario may be just the right amount of pressure to send them into distress.

Whatever the case may be, I want to paint a picture of grief that I think will help us to unlock some of the root causes for some of the battles we face in the mind. Some of what we experience is overlooked because often times, we go through the process of grieving too quickly, if at all.

When I think back, I can honestly say that I have felt distress over misplacing a wad of cash, losing my license and even missing out on certain opportunities. I start out in denial that what I had hoped to have or do is becoming impossible and then I move to anger because I would often wonder "Why this? Why now? Why me?" I wouldn't say that I enter into any degree of depression but often times I would become very sad and disheartened and with that last drop of hope I have in me; I would try to figure something else out to fix the problem. After I've done all I could do, the only thing left to do is accept it and all of this usually doesn't take beyond 12-24 hours to process through.

What distinguishes full on grief from this anecdotal unscientific and completely half-baked scenario is that grief *lasts*.

Somewhere along the way, society determined that some things in life you just have to "get over". Most people may consider it to be resilience to be able to carry on life as if nothing has ever happened after turbulent times and hurtful experiences, but resilience is actually the ability to heal and return to a normal state of health, mind and strength. Most of us persist in the direction away from the source of pain walking as if we are not wounded. For some reason, we don't think that it's dysfunctional to go about it this way. We prefer to call it dysfunction when someone persists in the same direction as the source of pain, expecting and hoping for something different. Even so, I don't think either of these options can ever yield the healing we seek.

To be hurt and not know why or not notice the pain develop may be more hopeless than to simply have an expectation that is delayed. It is startlingly normal to live with and within different types of grief, some of which will be discussed in this chapter. This section of the book is to serve as information and is not for the purpose of self-diagnosis, but I ask myself: what if the answer to our darkest moments is to be able to acknowledge trauma, identify grief, and grieve thoroughly to the point of acceptance and ultimately freedom?

I think it is incredibly easy to have experienced a traumatic event, particularly if the guardians of the home are victims of trauma themselves. Society has a way of fostering a sense of pride through media, music, and platforms given to people who do not understand their own need for healing. Blaming the victim and shaming the broken, consequently encourages people to try to live as though nothing can have a negative effect on them (while also slowly dying in the dark). It's equivalent to if someone was suffering a heart attack right before your eyes but insisted upon continuing life as normal.

What we don't necessarily know or realize is that along with some instances of trauma, one could also experience inhibited grief, no matter how much distance is created between self and the event. Inhibited grief occurs when an individual shows no outward signs of grief for an extended period of time. When a person is not allowed, or not allowing themselves, to process emotions thoroughly, the grief can be fairly undetectable but eventually can lead to physical manifestations and complaints that may be viewed as minor (i.e. feelings, nerves, pain, movement, sleep disturbance, anxiety, etc.). Just because this type of grief is invisible and inaudible to others, does that mean it is mild and harmless? Does that mean that the grief itself does not exist?

Think about it.

The Roots of Childhood

Though not fully transformed, society is changing in its approach to mental health; but it is not the most powerful influence on how we are shaped mentally and emotionally. To date, the most powerful influence on how we value our mental health lies within our childhood homelife, and it is within family where many of us have learned to bury and mask our emotions the most. Every adult was once a child and what I have noticed is that the children are the first to be negatively impacted by this manner of living. This is why our deepest digging often has to start in childhood with the experiences that were had in the home.

For example, if you grew up in a home where you received criticism or backlash for expressing sadness, disappointment, or anger even, you likely spend a portion of your life adapting to the restrictions of your environment. That may mean limiting self-expression even when your thoughts and feelings are overwhelming and explosive. Even as a child it may mean discovering and developing obscure and manipulative tactics to create an environment that is comfortable and suitable for you.

One can only imagine what this also means for that child when they become an adult. Those adaptive behaviors in childhood grow up to become maladaptive behaviors in society where you are remaining silent when you should be speaking up, exploding in anger at inappropriate times or becoming manipulative towards people you work with and those that you love.

Children are resilient, stemming largely from their hope. Children have access to something that is not a luxury to adults, and that is blissful ignorance. Young children have the capacity to continue in hope because they have not yet experienced the same terrible things happen repetitively, nor have they had the opportunity to see justice. Their ideas about what is right and wrong, good and evil exist, but they are not cognitively developed enough to perceive a traumatic event as it is happening. They don't recognize cruelty and abuse as much as they do fear and pain, but they can have memory of the fear and the pain and still have hope because they have not lived long enough to recognize the full extent of their experience.

Still, and again, every adult was once a child. So, what happens is as children grow and notice a pattern in other people and even themselves, a truth starts to form about their expectations versus reality. Bit by bit, the world that they lived in is built by their imagination and their ignorance is deconstructed and replaced by what keeps persisting in their lives. Sooner or later the good things that they expected out of life start to fall through at some point. Children start to recognize their wants and needs and therefore unknowingly develop expectations.

As adults, we know that there are times where you do not receive everything that you desire, or even need. However, for children there is a process that they go through to learn this facet of life. That process involves disappointment, and a lot of it. A healthy amount of disappointment for a child includes not getting a toy that he or she desperately wanted or having their less than favorite meal for dinner and being required to eat all of it. Being required to miss a few events or parties and being held accountable for poor behavior are all healthy for children as they learn to be functional in society.

However outside of such disappointments as these (and sometimes within these disappointments) there stands opportunities for trauma when you factor in elements of cruelty, repetition, bullying, abuse, and overall abruptness. Some desires we have though are appropriate, and when they are not fulfilled, disappointment is close behind. Not every disappointment leads to grief, but sometimes disappointment *can* feel a lot like loss. Furthermore, depending on how traumatic that loss was, people may enter into grief and ultimately begin to lose the childlike parts of themselves that has the courage and nerve to hope.

If children are repetitively and brutally forced into secrecy, learning to pretend to be okay when they are not, they are inevitably susceptible to suffer trauma and silently enter into a developed grief later in life. That grief remains silent until it is manifested into a more noticeable, physical challenge with day-to-day functioning – this is called masked grief. Masked grief is when there is impairment to normal functioning but the traumatized adult is unable to recognize that their dysfunctional behaviors or their aggressive symptoms are related to the loss or experience.

Journal Entry:

Reflect on your childhood.

What details do you remember about your being a child?

How do you feel about the details you were able to recall?

Arrested Development

Perhaps in our adulthood, what we grieve most is not the loss of a particular person, place or thing, but rather the loss of hope. Needless to say, many of us are roaming the earth, making decisions, creating families, and gaining profits, but not thriving. Many people are traumatized, grieving, and ultimately functioning at the same emotional, physical, and mental level that they were at the time of the first psychological injury. The issue is that we don't notice those who are traumatized and grieving until it collides with other issues of life and severely impacts their ability to function from day to day. They are heart sick and nobody knows it, not even themselves. Feeling "stuck" is a great indicator of when something is wrong.

Do you feel stuck?

It helps a lot to call the situation what it is, not attempting to appear to be okay or lying to others to make them feel comfortable. When on the track to healing, it is important to assess where you are in your process as you decide on where you would like to eventually be.

While there are said to be five to seven stages of grief (depending on the model you reference), it is not guaranteed that a person should experience all five stages or within any particular order. In addition to the fact that progressing through grief is not always linear, it is also possible to get stuck in one of the stages hindering the person grieving from ever reaching acceptance of the loss and thriving in other areas of life and development.

The model I am using to show the five stages of grieving are from author and Swiss-American psychologist Elisabeth Kübler-Ross. Information on grief helps to narrow down where a person is on the spectrum of their own experience. From there, it is good to refer to the scriptures for direction on how to navigate from one state to the next. It all goes back to the topic of truth. When we look at the truth of our own experience, scripture gives us access to see how it aligns to what we believe to be true about Jesus, the Gospel, and the Word of God.

Denial

One must cross over a river of pain in order to get to the land of healing. You don't have to go up the river, but you do have to cross it. Denial, however, is refusal to get into the water. It is resistance to accept that wrong has been done or loss has been experienced. Without using the term *denial*, we have discussed the relevance of this concept from early on in this book as we discussed the role that *your truth* plays in your healing. Elongated existence in this stage locks us away from healthy processing and progression into a liberated future. Denial much like a mental isolation from the pain associated with loss. Just like denial may create distance between a person and their pain, it can also isolate a person from their conscious self, from community, from God, and all that is needed to fully recover.

When stuck in the stage of denial, there may also be a resistance toward anyone or anything that would pull undesirable memories to the surface. It can become difficult to establish deep community with others or pray specific prayers because that all requires intimacy and confrontation with the abandoned parts of oneself.

If you believe you're stuck here, ask yourself:

- Are there others in my community who share my experience?
- Why is it hard to talk about my experience?
- What has been a result of my denial so far?
- Do I believe that Jesus knows what I am feeling?

Anger

It is not uncommon for victims of loss to exist in the stage of anger for a long time after the loss of a loved one, loss of hope, or distressing disappointment. Anger is one of those feelings that people tend to deny. Have you ever noticed rage in someone and then heard them try to convince you that they weren't angry?

Question: *What's wrong with being angry?*

Anger is a basic human emotion. It is supportive in basic human survival and serves as an instinct for our protection. This is why at the base layer of anger, there is always another more undesirable feeling. It may be sadness, fear, disappointment, a sense of being threatened or some other painful sense that is attached to and fueling the anger. Anger becomes problematic only when there is a lack of self-awareness of those root feelings or lack of strategy on how to control and resolve it. Within the process of grieving, anger is more complicated because there may not be a direct offense to which we can trace the anger, but we can dig until we perhaps discover a potential root cause.

Anger can be at its strongest toward people of authority because of the imbalance of power. That imbalance of power requires that the weaker rely on, trust and be subject to the stronger entity. We see this dynamic between children and parents, citizens and the law, students and teachers, and particularly between man and God. Those with less power are involuntarily dependent on the one with more power to meet certain needs, follow through with promises and perform in their leadership with due diligence, truth and safety.

Many people become angry with parents, family, leaders, and God when trust is broken and the relationship no longer feels safe. Some people develop an overall anger toward all authority once noticing a pattern of broken trust and insufficient protection with multiple different figures of power. The conflicting part of this anger is that though the anger exists, it may still be suppressed because the weaker entity is also not in a position to hold those in authority accountable. Additionally, the cultures that we are often raised in use the biblical principle of *honor* to protect leaders from being exposed in their wrongdoing. Therefore, some will try to resist feelings of anger on the premise of owing more powerful persons immunity, absolution and honor through silence. Again, anger is suppressed.

Sometimes, people are angry with themselves. The Apostle Paul describes it as a law within the members – or the body (Romans 7:21-25), where the desire is there to do one thing, but the power to do it is lacking. Surely anger toward self is just as, if not more, significant as anger toward others and should be acknowledged on the journey to healing. The Bible tells us to be angry but urges us not to sin and to not let the sun go down on that anger (Eph 4:26). If we are encouraged to let anger go quickly, then that would highlight the tremendous necessity to be aware of when we are in a state of anger.

Anger does not have to be wildly explosive, but it if it is suppressed and ignored, it becomes very difficult to progress out of it. Dealing with anger requires first confronting yourself about what you're feeling before confronting anyone else.

Ask yourself:
- Am I angry? With whom?
- Have I ever felt betrayed or abandoned by people I trusted?
- Am I angry with myself about anything?
- What did I expect God to do at my lowest point?

Bargaining

Bargaining involves making compromise or entertaining ideas that would alleviate the weight of grief. If there are any other possible outcomes, this involves exploring options to exchange one outcome for another. Essentially, we are thinking in terms of how a situation would not be a grievance *if only I could think of an alternative solution.* In effort to negotiate the pain away and avoid suffering, you may be existing in a headspace that is neither faith nor reality. In that moment, there are all sorts of betting, delaying, changing the subject, and anything else that would help you to avoid the fear the possibly of drowning in the pain.

If you believe you're stuck here, ask yourself:
- What do you fear most? Why?
- If you could control the outcome, what would it be? Could you be certain that nothing else would go wrong?
- Is there any part of you that is unsure about trusting God with the outcome of your life? Why?

Depression

Who are you? Do you know?

There are multiple aspects of our personality that makes us who we are. Our interests make us who we are. Our sense of humor makes us who we are. Even our pet peeves and aversions make us who we are. All of these dimensions of self are the foundations for the relationships we have, the communities we are a part of, the careers we pursue and the life we want to live – even the life that God has ordained us to live. From beyond childhood, these dimensions of our personality are informed partially by genetics and environment but is largely informed by God-given design. Usually, you like what you like and desire what you desire for the purpose of attracting you into your destiny.

Then, life happens and you are challenged to keep alive the things that make you *you* while also fighting the thoughts, feelings and emotions that you sense, but are not quite... you. What do you do when you don't feel like yourself? What most people do is suppress the thoughts, feelings, and emotions that are not consistent with their personality or who they desire to be. Perhaps anger is often suppressed because nobody is born angry and nobody wants to be angry.

Nobody wants to be discouraged.
Nobody wants to be doubtful.
Nobody wants to be afraid.

So, what does everybody do? *Suppress.* Pretend you are not in pain. Speak the opposite of what you feel, right? Especially when coming from a broken home, negative emotions can be tiresome. However, pretending they don't exist isn't how to overcome them.

Negative emotions are not *who* we are, but how we address them helps to establish who we are mentally, emotionally, and spiritually. Without negative emotions, positive ones have no context and we have no story. What is forgiveness without anger? What is courage without fear? What is hope without failure? Suppressing negative emotions removes the stepping-

34

stones that we need in order to reach who we desire to be. By removing those stepping-stones through suppressing negative emotions and events, the paradigm of our conscious being loses structural support.

Eventually, we may graduate from only suppressing negative emotions to also suppressing positive ones out of fear. We may suppress hope to avoid disappointment. We may suppress joy to avoid jolting pain. Amid the habit of suppressing every emotion, pretending it doesn't exist, there is inevitable exhaustion. There is guaranteed discouragement. There is definite confusion. Although the emotions are suppressed, existential questions are persistent until the light of everything that was once important seems to dim. Depression is a dark realm where everything regarding self has been suppressed to the point of inactivity.

Hope is the source that gives life and meaning to your desires and aspirations. Hope gives validity to what you deem to be important, true, and relevant. Without hope, nothing that empowers self is important, nothing that validates self is true, and nothing that has to do with health of self is relevant. Depression is that sense of nothingness.

If you believe you're stuck here, ask yourself:
- Who am I?
- What would your ideal life look like?
- What are you grateful for in your current reality?
- Do you know anybody who shares the same interests that you have/used to have?
- Do you believe that God has a purpose for your life? What do you know about it?

Acceptance

Acceptance is a state of being able to reconcile with the past or present and embrace the future. It is adopting a calm, retrospective view on a loss and maintaining stability in thoughts and emotions. Acceptance can only yield true healing if it involves the thorough work of acknowledging that an event occurred without the sense of *giving up* or trying to influence the situation – which is essentially still bargaining. Acceptance implies having no desire to change circumstances because they are issues of the past. This manner of acceptance allows you to recover from the lasting effects of the disappointment and allows you to have hope for the future.

Ask yourself:
- If you could change one thing about past disappointments or losses, what would it be?

Complications to Grief

Dr. Kübler-Ross later updated her model to include two additional stages including a first stage of Shock and a stage before Acceptance, called Testing which involves a seeking for ways to cope and recover from the damage incurred by the loss.

I have included these stages of grief, not to get technical with the psychology of it all, but rather to use it as a platform to highlight the extent to which grief may be felt. I am grateful for the added stage of grief called Testing, because I think it reflects where many people are right before they find true freedom. There are many criticisms to this model, one of them being that grief itself does not have stages, but symptoms. I think that can be substantiated just based on the fact that many who are grieving can be both depressed and angry at the same time. I would also even say that some of you who are reading this book are in the *Testing* stage while also maybe existing in the realm of depression, anger, and bargaining as well.

These stages of grief are one of the many ways that mental health advocates have tried to make sense out of the process in and out of human despair. Yet, because humans are so incredibly complex, it is impossible to fully resolve the issues of life through only science and research. Even within the scriptures the prophet Jeremiah speaks about the human heart asking, *"who can know it?"* Nonetheless, with this information you can name the state that you may be in at this season of your life and then determine what you need most from there to reach the place of healing.

In addition to the multiple coexisting stages of grief, there are endless types of grief and probably countless more yet to be discovered. The truth about grief is that nobody gets to determine that you are not grieving based on their assessment of your experience. In fact, the type of grief in which a person's society or culture makes them feel as though their loss or grief is insignificant or invalid is called *disenfranchised grief.*

I believe in the likelihood that many are even suffering from *complicated* grief. Complicated grief occurs when grief is combined with other mental conditions such as depression and anxiety. In this manner of grief, the responses to loss are long lasting and impact your participation in everyday activities. Complicated grief may be identified through identification of other types of grief (e.g. distorted grief, chronic grief, and delayed grief) but all this essentially shows the many modes of grief that a human can experience. This also supports the idea that much of our nation's widespread mental illnesses are likely rooted in unacknowledged and untreated grief.

Journal Entry:

In which, if any, of the 7 Stages of Grief, would you say you are existing?

Why?

Weakness

Sickness and weakness often go hand in hand with many heart diseases. Some people respond to weakness that comes with progressed sickness in fear that they are withering away unto death. Others anxiously anticipate their healing and ability to move around again. Some take each moment of weakness with sorrow and disbelief that their body could possibly feel what it feels while others may feel a great deal of shame for not maintaining daily healthy habits which would prevent their condition. One main symptom of a sick heart is emotional, mental, and spiritual weakness.

The Room Called Weakness

Fear, anxiety, sorrow, disbelief, and shame; it's so true that in times of weakness, we are susceptible to feeling one, all, or any combination of these feelings. When I visualize weakness, I see it as not only a feeling, but a place. If I were to visualize weakness, I would illustrate it as a room situated somewhere between the soul and the spirit. The walls are gray and the ceiling is low and all that one can do once they enter is collapse to the floor with their face to the ground. I see the walls of this room with mountings on it that represent unresolved memories, experiences, and history— and surrounding the person who enters are all of the very present thoughts and feelings about those experiences.

Anger walks laps around the person in weakness whispering *you're angry and have a right to be.*

Fear walks circles around them saying *you know you're just going to get hurt again?*

Shame walks around as well whispering *what makes you think you deserve anything from God?*

Disbelief adds *if God exists, then, where is He?*

Anxiety, sorrow, depression, denial and other relevant feelings all come to the person louder than before and because the whispers are *so* real, and so appropriate, by the time the whispers stop, they start to sound like the truth. Just as sure as these thoughts come resounding in the sound of your own voice, they eventually come out of your mouth. Soon, these lies become *your truth* and your confession represents your agreement with it.

Pivotal things happen there because it is a place of immense vulnerability. It can produce testimony and hope or it can multiply pain and suffering, it all depends on how you use the space. In many circles of faith, there may be confusion and insensitivity around how one can believe in Jesus yet *still* exist in deep realms of darkness and weakness. In this chapter, we will explore what it means to feel weak and be *in* weakness as well as how to maneuver through it.

Did you know that the Bible refers to us, humans, as being in the likeness of temples?

Do you not know that your bodies are temples of the Holy Spirit, who is in you, whom you have received from God? You are not your own.
1 Corinthians 6:19

"When an impure spirit comes out of a person, it goes through arid places seeking rest and does not find it. Then it says, 'I will return to the house I left.' When it arrives, it finds the house unoccupied, swept clean and put in order.
Matthew 12:43-44

When we first accept Jesus, we receive his Holy Spirit and the Holy Spirit dwells in us making our bodies as temples. In this body, the Temple of God's spirit, there are many rooms and several spaces that hold memories, history, and experiences. When we receive Jesus, He provides us His Holy Spirit, and the Holy Spirit dwells in us – let's say, He gets a room in our house. Now, just because the Holy Spirit dwells in our temples, that does not mean that every other room with its history and memories has suddenly disappeared or lost its influence on how we view and process life. There are still very present struggles within us that we have to actively welcome the power of Jesus to come in and correct.

If Jesus is real and the Holy Spirit is here in my body, then why does weakness continue to affect me in this way?

Here's how:

The Holy Spirit has functions, gifts and power to help us through life and to help us remain reconciled to the Father by changing the way we think, speak, and believe. Through the Spirit of God, we acquire wisdom, understanding, counsel, fortitude, knowledge, piety, and fear of the Lord (Isaiah 11:1-2). It is only by the Spirit of God that we are able to come to know and fear God. The Holy Spirit helps to learn more about the Lord and ourselves through the Word. This is only the foundation of our acquaintance with Him.

Receiving salvation and the Holy Spirit equips us to make the decisions we need to make in order to grow in understanding and to fight in the war against our own lives. The Holy Spirit is a comforter, a teacher, and a helper, among other things - but naturally there is still work to be done after the Holy Spirit comes in. The Holy Spirit has a room to start and through our walk with God, we start to invite Him into the other dark spaces of our house to which we need Him to bring His light. When the Holy Spirit begins to dwell in us, we are then empowered and encouraged to honor God with our bodies (1 Cor 6:20), be renewed in our minds (Eph 4:23), and work out our salvation with fear and trembling (Phil 2:12).

The will of God is not that we continue to ask Him to save us, because through faith and confession, salvation is already established. The will of the Father is that we use the Word of God to understand the nature of our battles and to fight effectively. With wisdom and understanding, we can read the Word and apply it to our lives and discover what is deeply broken about us. Through the counsel of the Holy Spirit, we are able to sift through confusion to fight with strength in the fear of the Lord.

A lot of times, when we enter into the place of weakness, we only come out weaker, but the Lord makes a promise in the scripture that reflects that weakness can actually transform into strength. The Apostle Paul testified about his own weakness saying:

Three times I pleaded with the Lord to take it away from me. But he said to me, "My grace is sufficient for you, for my power is made perfect in weakness." ...For when I am weak, then I am strong
2 Corinthians 12:8-9 (Edited)

In this story, Paul is telling us about an exchange He had with the Lord where he had an infirmity that he called a *thorn in his flesh*. He does not describe exactly what the suffering is, but Paul says that he pleaded three times that the Lord take it away from Him. Instead of taking it, the Lord responded with a weapon that Paul was to hear and take literally, "my grace is sufficient for you, for my power is made perfect in weakness". From this Word, Paul changed his language regarding His weakness and *because* the Lord told him that His power was made perfect in weakness, Paul went on to make a celebration of the very same weakness.

How much faith did it take for Paul to see his weakness as a point of strength simply because the Lord promised Him that His grace was enough?

If I were to apply this principle to my life, I would have to view weakness a bit differently. It challenges me to believe that the Lord has provided help and grace that causes me to progress, in spite of the experiences that broke me. The way I relate to weakness would then have to change to reflect my faith that the Lord's grace is sufficient as well as to provide the Lord opportunity to prove that His word is true!

Embracing Weakness

---

*My grace is sufficient for you, for my **power** is made perfect in weakness*

To those who do not experience the power of God, the power of God does not exist, unless they have faith. To change the way we see weakness into a matter of receiving grace is an act of faith. I believe that the true meaning of this scripture is best revealed though experience, but the way this scripture comes to life is by believing that there is power with which the Lord wants us to make acquaintance in the moments that we feel most weak. If we believe that, the way we enter the space of weakness will begin to change.

You may have once been advised to pull yourself together, get over it, and pull yourself out of darkness, but even that approach to weakness is merciless and unyielding. In fact, this approach is anti-Christ. The worst thing that could have ever infiltrated the faith of believers of Jesus is the idea of *will power*. Will power is an over-reliance on the notion that one can overcome weakness by the position of his or her mindset. Mind over matter, though it can appear to be effective and empowering, requires so much dependence on self that in times of weakness, it often fails to provide enduring strength.

This gaping loophole was created by the cultural approach to Christianity that embraced Jesus for His salvation but rejected the *actual* need for Him when it comes to even the seemingly minor decisions. Our decisions in seed form are planted when we make commitments and then grow into a forest of whatever that seed was destined to provide. Truthfully, we must rely on Jesus for everything down to who we date, where we live, our careers, and so much more because when we make commitments in these areas of life, it determines our environment and destiny as well as the environment and destiny of our children.

We receive Jesus's salvation, but do not receive His grace. We receive His salvation but adhere to *thou shall not's* rather than wading in a relationship with Jesus that goes beyond what you can do to prove you are actually saved. After practicing and excelling *doing right*, we typically get so drunk off the futility of our pseudo-perfection that we actually begin walking in pride. We begin to think we are stronger than we actually are and that it was through our will power we became righteous and qualified for salvation. In this practice, we may acquire a spotless track record for a season, but consequently we become trained to rely on ourselves to not only be righteous, but to also be strong. It's not until we find ourselves in this room called weakness again that we feel defeated and hopeless because in that moment the truth about our abilities are exposed.

Depending on the church and home environment through which you learned Christ, the first few to several years of faith is easily spent identifying as a Christian but not acknowledging the depths of your need for Jesus when it comes to day to day thoughts, feeling, and decisions. In that case, salvation is less a testimony of grace and more an arrangement where we secure our eternity and squander the time and space that we are allotted for now. Essentially, we are telling Jesus, *Save me, but leave my life up to me. I know what I want, I know what I don't want. I got it from here.* This mindset is precisely why most Christians struggle when their belief and their reality are in conflict. This mindset is also the reason we are warned in scripture that whoever lives his life trying to find his life will lose it, but whoever loses His life for the sake of Christ will find it (Matthew 16:25).

How then do we get from this self-reliant mindset to the sentiments in scripture where we are gleefully discovering where our limitations are and saying, 'I *will boast in my weakness!*'?

The entire purpose for receiving Jesus was for reconciliation to the Father, salvation unto eternity and to encounter His transformational power in our now.

True forgiveness requires Jesus because in our pain and weakness, we are incapable. Holiness requires Jesus because in our flesh, we are incapable of remaining consistent. We find that the Lord even leads us to pursue career and relational paths that will require that we rely on Him for provision and success. Likewise, He may steer us away from careers and paths knowing that we will have to walk by faith and not by sight in order to have the most powerful outcome. This room called weakness is a required space for us to encounter and recognize the redemptive power of God. Will power does not provide space for God to be involved to demonstrate *His power*, making Jesus' sacrifice and the return of the Holy Spirit irrelevant and useless to the person who rejects it.

However, if we enter the place of weakness again, on the belief that His grace is sufficient, there can be a testimony of Jesus. I imagine that the room would still look the same. The walls are still gray and the ceiling is still very low. By virtue of the meaning of weakness, once you enter, you'd still find yourself on the floor with your face to the ground. The walls would still be decorated with unresolved memories, experiences, and history, and around the person would still be all of the very present thoughts and feelings about those experiences. The difference, however, would be what you do with your face to the ground and your willingness to soak and boast in your weakness with holy expectation.

At that point, the direction of your thoughts and your reliance would be so rooted in your faith that it provides Jesus an opportunity to demonstrate His power. That power is the source of hope and expectation. The evidence of God's power looks different depending on the area of weakness, but with reference to the 7 spirits of God that now live inside of us, we are destined to leave the room with access to more wisdom, more understanding, more counsel, strength, knowledge, piety, and fear of the Lord.

Enduring in Weakness

Sometimes, I feel weak *all* day.

Angry *all day*.
Afraid *all day*.
Anxious *all day*.

Sad *all day.*

Eventually, I began trying to incorporate into my life the rationale that if I am going to be afflicted by my weakness all hours that I am awake, then I may as well spend as many of those hours as possible confronting my weakness head on. Recognizing weakness is one thing. Embracing weakness is another but enduring in weakness is where we are most strengthened. If the strength of God is made perfect in our weakness, then it is implied and proven that the longer we remain in weakness yearning for and embracing grace, the more strengthened we can become.

Memorizing scripture has culturally been used to manipulate people groups and shape the appearance of our righteousness, but the most effective use of scripture is in how much we are able to allow it to transform us. Our knowledge of Jesus and the scripture is best put to use in times of weakness because it is the most effective way to lean into the truth of Jesus, in *addition* to prayer itself. Prayer is communication with God but enduring in weakness may not involve any words at all.

The concept of will power is partially connected to what we value as subjective truth. When there is a gap between what we believe and what we see, we tend to close the gap by asserting our view or perspective as a truth to support our understanding of the circumstance. If we are ever able to create a degree of separation between our experience and our truth, it provides opportunity to see God add to our experience and therefore change what we call truth. Within that degree of separation, is the space to acknowledge that not everything that we see is as it appears and that there may even be a war that exists in spiritual realms that make our experience in weakness even more difficult.

You may have heard it said that in issues of mental health, the mind is at war with itself. However, if I'm trusting in the Word of God, I would also wonder if it is possible that my mind is at war with something else other than itself.

For we wrestle not against flesh and blood, but against principalities, against powers, against the rulers of the darkness of this world, against spiritual wickedness in high places.

Ephesians 6:12

If this scripture is not factored into what you call *your truth*, that leaves opportunity to blame yourself and others for conditions that actually stem from principalities, powers, rulers of darkness of this world and spiritual wickedness in high places. It requires as much faith to believe in the goodness of God as it does to believe that there is wickedness in the earth, but this only validates more the need to endure in the place of weakness <u>with</u> Jesus. His power is all the more necessary. The belief and understanding that my mind is not only possibly at war with itself, but even more likely in war with things that rule in the spirit realm leads me to remember why Jesus said *I give you power and authority to tread upon snakes, scorpions and all power of the enemy (Luke 10:19).*

The more you believe the principle represented in scripture that we have power over the works of the devil, the more equipped you are to endure in the room called weakness. The more you have written, bookmarked, or memorized the scripture, the more tools you have access to for meaningful endurance. In this space, it is essential that you recognize what you feel, but now you can do more than *just* feel. You can also fight from an endless source of perfected strength.

When we enter into the space of weakness, we are there with all of the very present thoughts and feelings about those experiences and they do continue to roam. However, our experience is different as we enter this room planning to linger, endure, and wrestle.

Yea, though I walk through the valley of the shadow of death, I will fear no evil: for though are with me: thy rod and thy staff they comfort me.

Psalm 23:4

Anger walks laps around you but because you believe the word of God, your prayer is founded on the promises of God. *Lord, I am crippled in anger – I need your grace to help me forgive and move past this so that I can move forward. I trust you to help me move forward.*

Fear walks circles around you, but because the Holy Spirit taught you the truth through the Word you can speak back and pray *God has not given me the spirit of fear, but power, love and a sound mind. Fear, I resist you and command you to leave me in the Name of Jesus!*

Shame walks around you as well, whispering but in remembering the Word you can say *there is therefore now no condemnation to those who are in Christ Jesus, His grace has saved me, not even my works! Every tongue risen in judgement against me shall be condemned in Jesus name!*

Your faith causes you to stay, and press, and persist there until you receive your breakthrough but all the while you will have relied on pure belief that Jesus has to work. If my weakness can persist for hours in a day even to the point of keeping me from sleeping in the night, then the one or two hours that I spend pressing into my belief that Jesus is a deliverer is all the more worth it.

Before you know it, that space called weakness is more so a space that is called *The Secret Place* (Psalms 91), where we find strength and peace. In that secret place you are resisting the devil and leaning on the word of God. In those serious moments of leaning into the Lord, it can feel like you are there for a long time. Nonetheless, the building up of your faith over time allows you to stay there knowing that the Word of God is true and that His grace truly is sufficient.

Submit yourselves, then, to God. Resist the devil, and he will flee from you.

James 4:7

Journal Entry:

Read Psalms 91.

What do you normally feel in times of great weakness? How do you typically respond?

Connecting the Dots

Fun fact about me: I am very nerdy about science and experimentation. In fact, I am secretly proud of it. I'm so nerdy, that after my husband and I got married, I had to fight every urge to watch an informative documentary on the mechanics of sex and the process of reproduction. I hope I haven't made you too uncomfortable to continue reading, but it connects, I promise. Let's move on.

In the previous chapter, we looked at seven stages of grief: shock, denial, anger, bargaining, depression, testing, and acceptance. My hope is that this chapter will help readers who are in the testing stage. The testing stage is described as the point where victims become aware that they have to somehow abort the cycle of vacillating between the four stages of grief outside of *acceptance*. Testing is where the person may begin experimenting with methods to find freedom and move on from the bondages that come with trauma and loss. If you have made it to this chapter, then you have reached the most important part of this book because this is where we connect the dots between loss of hope and finding it again through faith.

To the Jews who had believed him, Jesus said, "If you hold to my teaching, you are really my disciples. Then you will know the truth, and <u>the truth</u> will set you free."

Now a slave has no permanent place in the family, but a son belongs to it forever. So, if the Son sets you free, you will be free indeed.

John 8:31-32; 35-36

Why Jesus?

In addition to academic fields, humans seek, study and experiment with an array of topics, philosophies and ideas in order to get definitive answers to unending questions. Since before biblical times, man has experimented with religion, logic, spiritualism: Astrology, diviners, fortune tellers, and even witches to get answers to certain questions and determine their future. I would be remised to not acknowledge that there *is* power in some of these sources if one was to commit to tapping into the spiritual laws that are at work at the foundation of a religion or belief system.

In principle, much of what you find within various belief systems are consistent with pockets of scripture because spiritual principles do work if the person using them are knowledgeable of spiritual laws. These sources bring you all sorts results, but they cannot deliver the seeker from eternal bondage neither do they provide true healing for the sick heart. I'm here to tell you that after you have faced the truth regarding your existence and discovered how broken you really are, the answer is Jesus as the promises are true that who Jesus sets free is free *indeed (John 8:36)*.

All the advice you receive has made you tired. Where are all your astrologers, those stargazers who make predictions each month? Let them stand up and save you from what the future holds. But they are like straw burning in a fire; they cannot save themselves from the flame. You will get no help from them at all; their hearth is no place to sit for warmth.

Isaiah 47:13-14

Sometimes we think we *have* tried Jesus, not realizing that what we had spent years saying, doing and repeating wasn't about Jesus – instead it had all been religion. As followers of Jesus, we teach and subscribe to spiritual principles that have to do with meditation, thinking, speaking, and faith, but the primary and essential difference is Jesus. We trust in the gospel of the Kingdom of God and therefore inherit the freedom that comes with Jesus both now and forever. A belief system that does not require submission to God can be spiritual and effective, but it cannot produce wholistic prosperity or eternal salvation.

Nonetheless, believing in Jesus is not just about what we believe God can do for us, it is even more so about becoming children of God! Did you know that not everyone is a child of God? Ephesians 2 talks a lot about what transformation comes with receiving Jesus. Before we were ever called *children of God*, we are originally *children of disobedience!* It is the state in which all of us were born. All of us were shaped by iniquity (Psalm 51:5) and all that we ever knew at one point in time was evil. Jesus knows this about us — that every person who was born must be born again to experience the supernatural process of adoption (Romans 8:15).

Wherein in time past you walked according to the course of this world, according to the prince of the power of the air, the spirit that now worketh in the children of disobedience: Among whom also **we all** *had our conversation in times past in the lusts of our flesh, fulfilling the desires of the flesh and of the mind; and were by nature the children of wrath,* **even as others**.

Ephesians 2:2-3

When we receive Jesus, everything changes from how we see ourselves to how we see others, and ultimately how we see God. This gospel gives us hope beyond the conditions of our home. We can look beyond the iniquity of our parents and begin to see the holiness of our Heavenly Father. We become free from the unrighteousness in our DNA and have access to the Blood of Jesus which cleanses us and with practice we learn how to look to Jesus for healing, comfort, assurance, and understanding rather than looking to others.

Now, I'm sure you still have a lot of questions.

If Jesus is so good, why would he allow me to experience what I've experienced?

Where was Jesus when I was being abused as a child?

Further in this book we will look at some reasonings to ponder. My hope is that by reading this book, your hunger is deepened to learn more. Everything you need to know is truly found in Jesus.

Where is Jesus?

Religion teaches the appearance of Jesus, and the appearance of what is holy, but it leaves out the very *heart* of God to His creation. The truth is that Jesus is sometimes nowhere to be found in the places that we tend to expect Him. People tend to look for Jesus in a church or in a song. They become confused when He is not in a man who calls himself a preacher or in a prophet. They become frustrated when He isn't where other people said He would be and suffer from even more loss of hope when He can't be felt or heard in times of turmoil and grief.

The first step in truly finding the healing that is in Jesus, is to begin to seek where He has laid Himself out in His Word. Literally, everything you need to know about the man, the Savior, that you hear so much about is in the Bible. Yet, so many people become satisfied with the church, the songs, the preachers, and the prophets and then resist and reject Jesus Himself when those substitutes don't follow through or hold up well under pressure. Although he was man, Jesus is nowhere near being *as* man. So, before any of us can receive from Him, we have to check our religion at the door with faith and honor knowing that He is not the idol hanging on the wall and that He requires that we seek Him.

And without faith it is impossible to please God, because anyone who comes to him must believe that he exists and that he rewards those who earnestly seek him.

Hebrews 11:6

The Kingdom of God is heavily dependent on the children of God living out His truth. You can imagine that this is why who we choose to have children with is so important. Choosing a partner that is a child of God determines what type of mother or father your children will have. The mother and father of a home are the guardians of their children's experience. When the parents and home is governed by godly principles, they are able to lessen (not erase) the trauma, sin, and depravity that the child grows up in.

God is not afraid of a sick heart. He is not waiting for you to appear to be healthy before He comes into your life. In fact, Jesus pursues us to heal us, make us new and to make us more like Him (not more like the pastor or the strongest prayer warrior you know). Jesus, He who is also the Spirit of God, is inside of those who welcome Him in faith. Jesus is inside of the parents, teachers, friends, and leaders that listen to Him. Our communities should reflect the number of people in our radius that have truly accepted Jesus and become children of God. If God were to force Himself on man, we would liken Him to a dictator. Jesus is waiting to be received.

Furthermore, Bible says exactly where He is and what He is doing for those who believe.

Who then is the one who condemns? No one. Christ Jesus who died-- more than that, who was raised to life--is at the right hand of God and is also interceding for us.

Romans 8:34

In another part of scripture it speaks to this placement of Jesus, being resurrected and seated at the right hand of The Father:

"... far above all rule and authority, power and dominion, and every name that is invoked, not only in the present age but also in the one to come. And God placed all things under his feet and appointed him to be head over everything for the church, which is his body, the fullness of him who fills everything in every way."

Ephesians 1:21-23

Now, Jesus, having all power in His hands, it would seem that if He is in Heaven interceding for us, everything should be all right and that there should not be so much pain in the earth, but that thinking does not take into account the purposes of God and His plan which has always been for man to have dominion over the earth and for His glory to be shown through them. God gave us the earth to roam and have for ourselves unto Him (Gen 1:26), but God's plan in its perfection became subject to something that even the church doesn't discuss: sin.

Children are sexually, mentally and emotionally abused because there is sin in the earth and Jesus is seated at the right hand of the Father waiting to be received and interceding for those who accept Him so that they can be empowered to effectively do something about it. *This* is where religion has misled generations of people who want to have a relationship with God but do not know why they feel so distant. Religion has taught us to sing, dance, shout, pray and recite sayings and scriptures expecting for something to happen as a result.

The relationship that Jesus wants with us is not one where we pray and He does things for us. The relationship He wants is one where we seek Him, and He does things *in* us. When Jesus does something *in* us, not only do we change, but we then begin to influence change in our environment. When we seek first the Kingdom of God, we can then carry the Kingdom of God into the earth. Religion never taught us this, but it is in the Word!

Romans chapter 8 speaks a lot about what it actually means to believe in Jesus and walk this walk of faith. I have included a few verses that prove that the will of God is that we be delivered from bondages and suffering so that we can be free *and* free others.

I consider that our present sufferings are not comparable to the glory that will be revealed in us. The creation waits in eager expectation for the revelation of the sons of God. For the creation was subjected to futility, not by its own will, but because of the One who subjected it, in hope that the creation itself will be set free from its bondage to decay and brought into the glorious freedom of the children of God.

Romans 8:18-21

The more we study the Word, the more we realize that there is actually a lot we don't know, but the Lord is a rewarder of those who diligently seek Him and those who trust in the Lord for salvation and restoration are the ones who see healing. Jesus is waiting for us to believe in Him like He believes in us. He sees every state of brokenness and offers healing. He acknowledges this sickness yet sees the end of it and beyond.

Because of religion, those who work the hardest to believe Him may still miss Him because they believe, but do not seek. Many people in church think they've found Jesus and no longer need to seek Him, keeping them in dangerous levels of ignorance. Nonetheless, those that seek Him will begin asking questions and finding answers in the Word.

Journal Entry:

What has changed about how you view Jesus and your faith?

Healing In Community

Jesus, He who is also the Spirit of God, is inside of those who welcome Him in faith. Jesus is inside of the parents, teachers, friends, and leaders that listen to Him. How hopeless is it when we look into our community and find that no one around us has invited Him in.

Many times, in trouble, it is natural to isolate − withdrawing from everyone to be in spaces that are filled with silence and mourning. Solitude is space wherein we are simply alone, but isolation is the space where we go to get *away* from the people around us. Solitude is healthy, but isolation is detrimental.

When you are surrounded by people who spew toxicity and hate, it can feel like the logical thing to isolate. When we are healing, it is essential to have that place of solitude so that we can speak to and hear from the Heavenly Father, but it is equally as important to be in a community of fellowship where others can teach you, speak faith over you, counsel, encourage and pray for you with precision and power as well. This is why it is so important to have teachers of truth in our churches, that help us see where the truth of our experiences fit with God's plan for salvation, healing and deliverance. Find a church that has a deliverance ministry and people who can pray and teach you how to address the spiritual agents that may be the cause of some of your afflictions.

(For the weapons of our warfare are not carnal, but mighty through God to the pulling down of strong holds;)

2 Corinthians 10:4

This scripture alludes to what is referred to as spiritual warfare. The Lord has equipped all of His children to engage in such warfare, but when you are in a place seeking healing, you will need a community that will listen to your experience with empathy yet also address strongholds, principalities, powers, and spiritual wickedness that you may not understand and cannot see.

Strongholds

The word 'stronghold' is a war term. A stronghold is a building that has been structured and built to prevent enemies from being able to attack a region (e.g. tower, castle, etc.). It's also defined as a place where a particular cause or belief is strongly defended or upheld. While this is a term used in natural terms, it is used in scripture to represent the spiritual happenings that occur in the mind of man.

In the spiritual sense, strongholds are built up and fortified by experiences, lies and partial or lack of biblical teaching. From the beginning of childhood, even through the disappointment, trauma, and confusion, the enemy begins to build strongholds in our minds. Parents, teachers, friends, and leaders who have received Jesus, and embraced the gifts of the Holy Spirit, are able to see the stronghold as it forms or before it forms. They are then able to teach, preach and pray in a way that *pulls down* the stronghold (1 Corinthians 10:4), but when your community is absent of people who are able to do that, the stronghold gets stronger by more experience and skewed reality.

At that point, what you confess as *your truth* then becomes the truth for you, but in the end only defends causes or beliefs that separate you from the truth of God.

Strongholds are a part of the reason some feelings and perspectives are so hard to shake and dispel. They were designed to be strong and withstand battle. The most exceedingly stubborn people you know, or those you may say are "ignorant", are likely dealing with a stronghold preventing them from receiving information from someone who disagrees with them.

For example, a stronghold that protects ideas of racism are built on anywhere from a few to many experiences that people have had with those of a particular race. In addition to that experience, a racist person may believe prejudgments and lies about people who have a specific racial identity marker. Without someone in the environment to teach the harm behind embracing these lies from early on, what the racist person believes to be true about a particular group of people rings to be true in their minds and behind this stronghold are spirits of hate, racism, fear, and perhaps a host of other unclean spirits. From there, the person afflicted with this stronghold will need to be renewed in the spirit of his or her mind through the truth, freedom, and deliverance of Jesus.

It can be confusing on how a person can believe in Christ *and* racist, but it is actually quite possible if the parents, teachers, friends, and leaders in that community are distracted by arguments rather than dealing with the stronghold through powerful teaching, preaching and prayer. Where there is a stronghold, there is likely a demon that needs to be cast out. That's a part of what the scriptures in Ephesians 6 and 2 Corinthians 10 speak to when they speak of war.

Now if we can look at the condition of a racist and understand how strongholds work, then we should be able to see how the strongholds in our own minds work as well. All of the work that went into addressing your feelings, your truth, and your trauma were for the purpose of seeing where strongholds had a foundation to form. Nonetheless, even if you discover that you have a stronghold, community is still quite necessary to lay hold of your complete freedom. The Lord designed us to need each other and work together for His glory to be revealed in us.

He makes the whole body fit together perfectly. As each part does its own special work, it helps the other parts grow, so that the whole body is healthy and growing and full of love.

Ephesians 4:16

In community is where God has placed His gifts of healing and the demonstration of His power.

There are different kinds of gifts, but the same Spirit distributes them. There are different kinds of service, but the same Lord. There are different kinds of working, but in all of them and in everyone it is the same God at work.

1 Corinthians 12:4-6

Community helps build our hope and bring us into healing because we can then add to our knowledge of Jesus and see the demonstration of Jesus alive in us.

Resources

In addition to that, if we look into our geographic community, we find resources that will help us to get along in everyday life. Reaching out to people who work in education or the career field that you are interested in are small steps to keep moving forward into your destiny. Therapists and counselors are available to help with sifting through the density of pain that we often experience in this life. Mental health professionals do a great work in exposing the paradigms in our thinking that need to be addressed and rehabilitated.

A lot of healing has to do with the mind and as a believer we are encouraged to be renewed in the spirit of our mind (Ephesians 4:23). This implies that there is work to be done in our minds both spiritually and naturally. We must ultimately return to the Father with whatever is discovered as we reach out to others and make use of the resources that are available to us, but the key factor is that people are better together. No one is ever truly successful without the help of *someone*.

If the Father designed us to be free and to free others through His power, healing must come from others in the earth and body of believers that He has empowered. It is extremely important to seek the Father for direction on where the community is that will help you find and walk in the healing that you need, as well as help you hope again.

Journal Entry:

What qualities and resources do you need in a community in order to feel adequately supported and covered?

Healing Through Prayer

Sometimes it is already difficult enough to find the time, language and strength to pray. Even for those who have known God, prayer can be the most difficult headspace to get to. The environment may just be *too* loud *all* the time. Sometimes we begin to feel unworthy to address the Lord and other times we just don't know how to find another way to say what we have already said.

When religion is our primary method to get to God, the first thing that is negatively impacted, besides our relationship with others, is our relationship with the Lord. When the relationship we have with Jesus is skewed or out of whack, our prayer life is sure to take a hit as well. In reality, no one takes on partnership in a relationship where there is always slow, awkward, and meaningless communication.

Some of us have prayed about the same things for a very long time but imagine this dynamic in the natural sense. If you are speaking to someone about the same thing over and over again and never see a change in their behavior or receive feedback on what you said, you would stop talking to that person. In the same sense, many of us struggle to continue to pray because we have prayed over and over again about the same things, but get no response, no feedback, and see no change. No wonder many people struggle with faith. Religion brings people to a place of constantly praying but does not sufficiently close the gap between God and those people.

With that gap being there, prayer doesn't happen the way that it should happen. It's almost as it would be praying to an image, or a statue-like idol, and then getting frustrated when the object is inanimate and powerless. Furthermore, it is incredibly frustrating for people who desire to believe God hear counsel from others that involves praying. Receiving counsel like that carries a presumption that whoever is afflicted has not already tried prayer. With that being said, this section of the book will come with dissecting prayer. Prayer is not a substitute to community, teachers, and mental health professionals, but rather is a healthier way to spend time when in solitude.

There is a *way* to pray, but it does not have to do with the way you sound, or the words you say. In the same way that many of us have to find our way out of dead religion into relationship, we also have to transition out of praying like "Christians" and into praying like "sons".

What do I mean by that?

There is a way that "Christians" pray. We hear them pray, we marvel at their eloquence and people honor them saying "I wish I could pray like that!" I don't mean this in a derogatory sense, but our reality is that the topic of prayer can often involve a lot of assumption and vanity. So, when I mention praying like a "Christian", I mean praying in alignment with the culture that is perpetuated in Christian circles. The way we pray should change over time, which reflects a moving, growing, living relationship with the Lord. Hearing, seeing, and being familiar with prayer may program us to believe that we know all that there is to know about it. This limits our seeking the Word for answers and then limits our ability to grow in the area.

What prayer sounds like in modern-day Christianity will vary considerably depending on the culture or denomination that you are or have been surrounded by. One way is not necessarily more right than the other, but the Bible, our primary source, tells us specifically not to pray like the hypocrites do.

And when you pray, do not be like the hypocrites, for they love to pray standing in the synagogues and on the street corners to be seen by others. Truly I tell you, they have received their reward in full. But when you pray, go into your room, close the door and pray to your Father, who is unseen. Then your Father, who sees what is done in secret, will reward you. And when you pray, do not keep on babbling like pagans, for they think they will be heard because of their many words. Do not be like them, for your Father knows what you need before you ask him.

Matthew 6:5-8

You may have seen this manner of prayer before, both in and outside of churches. You may have been the person to pray in this manner because it simply is what you always knew. The grace of God covers us for when we don't know any better and then brings us into the season of revelation and restoration. Nevertheless, to pray in this way is not how we deepen our relationship with God nor is it how we receive healing from the sick heart. Before we get into what it looks like to pray like the children of God, I want to emphasize the characteristics of prayer that we may be used to so that we can turn away from it and get into a habit of true, intimate communication with the Father. When the hypocrites pray:

- They never repent for anything; hence why they are called hypocrites
- They say what sounds nice. *"How you are supposed to pray"*
- They pray for selfish gain; with wrong motives (James 4:3)
- They pray as victims, lacking power because they know not the Source.

May those of you, who are reading this book, receive healing from your Heavenly Father as you approach Him in prayer. The only way to receive anything from your Heavenly Father, is to first opt into the *belief* that you <u>are</u> indeed one of the sons and daughters of God and then seek what it means to walk as such. It's not an issue to not have known what it means to live like a child of God. It's only a matter of being willing to learn.

For if you live according to the flesh, you will die; but if by the Spirit you put to death the misdeeds of the body, you will live. <u>For those who are led by the Spirit of God are the children of God.</u> The Spirit you received does not make you slaves, so that you live in fear again; rather, the Spirit you received brought about your adoption to sonship. And by him we cry, "Abba, Father." The Spirit himself testifies with our spirit that we are God's children. Now if we are children, then we are heirs— heirs of God and co-heirs with Christ, if indeed we share in his sufferings in order that we may also share in his glory.

Romans 8:13-17

So, if we are children of God, we are not only living a life that follows the Spirit of God, but we are also praying in a way that follows the leading of the Holy Spirit. The biggest step you can take in your walk with Jesus is to truly identify yourself as a child of God and then live, move, and pray as such. This step is the one that leads to a journey with a completely different destination than the one you had before. When you follow after the spirit of God and begin to learn what that means, everything changes, including your mind, body, and your will.

The mind houses your thinking. The body is your vehicle by which your soul and spirit move, and your will determines which way you will go in your everyday decisions. You will find that these three parts of yourself have to fully surrender to the Will of the Father in order to receive the knowledge, understanding and healing that He has for you. Prayer is the only place where some of the deepest levels of submission are accessed. Where there is submission there is transformation in the mind, soul, spirit and will.

Journal Entry:

What have been some of your biggest challenges in prayer?

Do you presently view yourself as a son or daughter of God?
Why or why not?

Healing Through Prayer: Repentance

If we trust in the scriptures, then we do trust that nothing, not even our sin can separate us from the love of God (Romans 8:35-38). In fact, Jesus did not wait until there was a person in the earth worthy of His crucifixion to die. It was while sin was still rampant in the earth that Christ died (Romans 5:8). As terribly wicked as we deem "these days" to be, they were not nearly as wicked as they were before Christ entered the earth. Things are actually better now than they were at the time that He died. This alone illustrates that God's love and sacrifice has never been in exchange for clean record or the absence of sin. In fact, our need for Him as a result of our sin is what has motivated His love.

Furthermore, in Genesis, when sin first entered the hearts of men, God's love persisted as he created a natural garment to cover their nakedness and prevent their shame. Later in scripture, far in the New Testament, we are encouraged to behave in the same manner toward one another.

Most important of all, continue to show deep love for each other, for love covers a multitude of sins.

1 Peter 4:8

Nonetheless, in the same chapter that Adam and Eve were covered after their transgression against God, their willful desire to disobey God still resulted in their separation from Him and removal from the garden of Eden. From there begins the story about a world rife with sin and the Father's plan of redemption to return mankind to the place of Eden. We cannot have the promises of God without returning to that original place of relationship and presence with the Father. True repentance is turning away from the history of disobedience to have agreement with God in the face of very present temptation.

Often when we you hear the word *repent*, it tends to come across as some sort of threat to people who presumably fear Hell, but repentance is not:

- asking for forgiveness
- regret
- shame

Repentance is having an intention and mindset to turn away from any way that does not line up with the Word and will of the Father. You can be a Christian for years and then find that there is a mindset, a conviction, a point of view, and of course sin that you need to repent from. Holding on to unbiblical views gets in the way of freedom and true joy in the Holy Ghost.

Repent ye therefore, and be converted, that your sins may be blotted out, when the times of refreshing shall come from the presence of the Lord.

Acts 3:19

Repentance goes far beyond apologizing for not keeping the ten commandments you learned about in Sunday School. It requires a journey with God in faith to really see the things in our lives that we need to turn away from in order to see Him more. Some may disagree about what necessitates repentance, but I no longer buy into the narrative that conversations about repentance itself makes people uncomfortable or offended. I believe that it is the selectivity around what people allegedly *"must"* repent from based on ideas that are not supported by scripture. For the most part, I think what makes people uncomfortable is the bullying and scolding that happens as people urge others to repent.

Nonetheless, we cannot have all of God, including His freedom, if we will not agree with what God says is good for us. All that pertains to life and godliness, is so that we can truly have all of God and that is why we must repent. What God says is good for man - in His laws and commands - are because He knows what gives the enemy access to our lives. God wants you free, so He says:

> *Repent! Agree with Me, believe on Me, let Me give you My Spirit and the inheritance of my Kingdom*

Healing Through Prayer: Surrender

As humans, after we live through a certain amount of trauma and disappointment, we soon develop standards and defenses to prevent the same things from happening again or having as much impact. These things do not prevent us from experiencing pain ever again, but it does give a sense of control and security with regard to our emotions and relationships. Some standards are conscious, while others are subconscious, but ultimately, we spend our lives adapting to our environment through our experiences and deciding how we will minimize the impact of possible future disappointment and trauma. Whether consciously or subconsciously, we are not only creating standards and defenses within our relationships with people, but we are also creating defenses within our relationship with God.

Typically, when we hear the word *surrender* it is with reference to giving up resistance when in a battle with an enemy. At that point, the person or team who surrenders is declaring that the opponent can determine the outcome and reward of the battle. The meaning of surrender in this context is not so different when we consider the fact that after we have experienced a number of negative things, a lot of what we begin to think about God is that He is in fact an enemy. It may take a while to admit it but we begin to see Him as the all-powerful God who could have stopped it, but instead, allowed people and circumstances to stress, abuse, and oppress us. At that point, we may consciously or subconsciously view God as an enemy making the idea of surrender appear daunting and outright stupid.

What sense does it make to surrender and submit to someone who supposedly loves me but didn't save me when I obviously needed Him to?

Surrender is most difficult when you're in a place of such anger, pain and sickness that your trust in the Lord has diminished. Nonetheless, before you can move forward in productive communication with God, one of the first things that will need to be restored is some sense belief in the Lord. What that essentially means is that all of the boundaries and defenses that have been set in place against God will need to be retired for the purpose of reconciling the relationship. There are certain things that we truly expect from God based on what we view the meaning of being a *good* God is. What we expect from God may not even be derived from scripture, but it is stamped as a on our hearts as a memory of each time that we expected something from God but He did not deliver.

One trap that people commonly fall into is believing that the access that we have to prayer is primarily to serve ourselves and get what we want or need – much like how people of polytheistic beliefs would pray to different gods for different specific resources such as rain, fertility, etc. As we mature in our relationship with God we realize that our hopes, though they might be good, do not always reflect God's purpose or His timing. We have to return to the scripture and the narrative of His promises to align the truth of our experiences to God's truth. Recognize that our priorities are not the same as the Lord's in that His first priority for us is secure salvation and separation from sin. His second priority is that we seek first the Kingdom of God and His righteousness. His third is that all things are added to us according to our need and finally as we continue to seek His plan for us, we can come into the manifestation of the abundant life that He has promised.

As children of God, that means that we have to be willing to forget what we so adamantly wanted before, lose anticipation about what will happen in the future, and trust so much in the Lord that you can value the Word of God despite what the conditions are right now in the present.

A lot of people very transparently confess to me saying *I don't know how to surrender* and it's nothing to be ashamed of. In fact, it's better to acknowledge that you may not know how to truly surrender than to assume that you are as surrendered as you could possibly be. Devoting time to the topic of surrender is necessary because the ability to surrender closes the gap between what you currently may experience with God and what you could potentially experience with Him.

We become angry at God largely because of how the sin of others has directly impacted us. The depravity and irresponsible behaviors of family, friends and romantic partners bring us to the brink of death and in our minds, God is the blame for not stopping their destructive behavior. When you are angry at God, it requires a leap of faith to be willing to start over with Him – or in other words, surrender everything that you have known or thought you knew in order to give Jesus a chance to write your story with Him at the very start of the narrative.

The story starts at salvation but it builds through the information that is available in the scripture and the notions of the Holy Spirit that we have access to after salvation. At no point should we feel that we know all that there is to know about God, but instead we benefit from being willing to restart from the beginning and check for cracks in our foundation.

Not that I have already attained, or am already perfected; but I press on, that I may lay hold of that for which Christ Jesus has also laid hold of me. Brethren, I do not count myself to have apprehended; but one thing I do, forgetting those things which are behind and reaching forward to those things which are ahead, I press toward the goal for the prize of the upward call of God in Christ Jesus.

Philippians 3:12-14

Surrender is not just for a particular time, in a particular season. In our relationship with the Lord, we must be ready to surrender our life. Your career, your marriage, your hopes for family and your expectations of friends all have to be completely given to the Father out of trust that He will cause all things to work together for your good. Your surrender has to be so deep and so thorough that you're okay with whatever the Lord allows you to go through in order to get to your destiny. True surrender is a matter of deciding that the Lord can be trusted to make something beautiful of the past, present and future outcomes of your life.

We tend to tell God what we desire and then expect Him to make it happen saying, "Lord here are my desires; you can do *whatever* you want to prepare me to receive them". This is partial surrender – if that. Total surrender is a matter of saying, "Lord, here is my life, you can do with it what You will". Surrendering all things is necessary because anything that is not surrendered has the potential to influence everything and resurrect old issues. For example, you are content with God's plan for your career but are not surrendered in the area of marriage, then what God desires for your career could produce conflict for the direction the Lord wants to take you for marriage.

Likewise, if you do not surrender your relationships and the outcomes that resulted from it, then those areas of hurt and resentment will dictate everything it can possibly touch and make it nearly impossible to move forward. Your future will be full of worry and paranoia while your present is paralyzed. If I could break the concept of surrender down into two parts, it would be in the areas of pride and unforgiveness. In effort to show you that surrender *is* possible, allow me to go into some detail about these two areas.

Do you see a person wise in their own eyes? There is more hope for a fool than for them.

Proverbs 26:12

Forgiveness

Forgiveness is a great sign of surrender because it involves *letting go* of how you feel and what you believe about a person who has harmed you. Forgiveness is completely countercultural, but the practice is life-giving. It involves making peace with the fact that there is nothing in me that can change the person or the circumstance that caused me to suffer. Surrender is an invitation to the Lord to make something beautiful out of the mess. Surrender is an act of faith that says that I *believe* He will give me beauty in exchange for these ashes (Isaiah 61:3) even if I take my eyes off the offense and the offender that railed against me.

I noticed that when people have the testimony of being able to forgive, the Lord is gracious to show revelation to pair with the instance of forgiveness. We forgive ultimately because Jesus instructs us to, but in addition to that:

- We forgive because we recognize that those who hurt us were broken themselves
- We forgive because we recognize the lesson that had to be learned through the experience
- We forgive because God has forgiven us.

Nonetheless, before any of us can get to the place of forgiveness, we have to confront whether or not it is in our *will* to forgive. If it is in your will to forgive, you have the keys to forgiveness. This does not mean that you are instantly happy about your experience or even that you are (or should be) reconciled. This only means that you are prepared to continually surrender the person who offended and hurt you even when you have the opportunity to be full of resentment.

Take a second to go back to that idea that you are a house. In your "house", each and every experience and relationship has a room and each room holds memories with specific individuals. In certain rooms, we can go in and find the individuals that we have loved the most and who have loved us. In those rooms, the walls are painted with bright and meaningful colors and you have mounted pictures of your fondest memories. The furniture is decorated with gifts, quotes and souvenirs and simply being in the room gives you immensely positive emotions.

Not every room in your house looks this way though. Some rooms are for individuals and experiences that have hurt us most. You can imagine what this room must look and feel like. The walls are painted with dimmer but equally as meaningful colors and the pictures on the wall are the memories that you wish you could forget. The only furniture there are pieces that represent the harm that was done to you and instead of mere quotes, there are loud mounted speakers through which you can hear the harsh words spoken over you. Further inside the room there is a cage, and that's where the person who hurt you lives.

Ideally, we could go into that room, see the aggressor in that cage, and begin to unleash well-deserved wrath. We feel anger and resentment. We feel regret for not defending ourselves and imagine what we could do now to the person in the cage to make up for it (bargaining). Sometimes it's multiple people in the cage: the one who hurt us and the one(s) who didn't stop it. Before we know it, we have spent hours, days, or weeks in a dark room with the person that hurt us (depression) and the weakening pain makes it extremely difficult to leave that room. The illustration of forgiveness is evident in how long you stay in this room and what you do while you are there. It may take a little while to actually grab the keys and unlock the cage door to let the prisoner out, but forgiveness starts in the decision to start renovating the room.

Imagine yourself repainting the walls in red to represent the blood of Jesus through which all sin is forgiven. Imagine replacing those pictures of most awful memories with ones of scriptures that teach us mercy. You take out every piece of furniture in that room, from the lightest to the heaviest, and replace it with articles of the secret place. You find sound system that blasted the sounds of your aggressor and switch the soundtrack to Psalms of David — both the lamentations and the songs of worship. Renovations can take weeks and sometimes months, but the Lord leverages your decision to start the project and provides grace to see the finished product.

The most essential ingredient to forgiveness is grace. Grace gives us the opportunity to have and do that which we naturally wouldn't be able to do and do not deserve. None of us deserve anything from the Lord considering we *all* have transgressed against Him. Grace to be saved is the beginning of our need, and grace to forgive is next in order since we must forgive in order to be forgiven. Therefore, if you have the will to forgive, the grace of God will give you the capacity to do so. The only thing that can stand in the way of forgiveness is self, which leads us into the topic of pride.

Journal Entry:

Who in your life do you have yet to forgive?

Write a letter of forgiveness to each person.

Pride is the number one resistance to all things godly, especially surrender and forgiveness. Often times, we become victims of loss or trauma before we are even old enough to know what is happening to us. As we get older and gain acuity, we discover the pleasure of figuring out who we are, what we like and what we dislike. In this stage of discovery, speaking *your* truth takes on a whole new meaning.

Our nature is emboldened more than ever before and we determine where we will stand in reference to the people and experiences that surround us. We determine what we want and need out of friends and partners and we gain ambitions about careers and standards of living. As children, we may waver more or less in what we allow in our space in terms of friends, depending on your personality and we certainly accept more toxic behaviors from family or repeat aggressors. As adults, we are able to narrow in on what we want, what we don't want, what we will and will not allow and how we feel about specific types of people. Ultimately, our thoughts take shape to reflect a very strong perspective that is shaped by our experiences.

To understand the danger of pride, we have to go back to its original definition. The modern concept of pride is generally perceived as very harmless. It is parallel to dignity, honor, and self-respect. When in respect to movements such as Black Pride, or LGBTQ Pride, it is defined as having deep pleasure or satisfaction with one's own achievements and qualities. For marginalized and disenfranchised groups, movements that emphasize pride in social identity are for the purpose of rebounding from the negative, harmful, violent, and deprecating responses that they have received from the greater portion of society. Groups that share an identity, experience, or culture find empowerment in gathering together in one spirit to take pleasure in who they are even while the overwhelming majority of their surrounding communities show hate, disapproval, and disgust for their identity.

Consider there is an imaginary line that represents a certain standard of quality of life. Imagine that everyone in society has the luxury of living up to an equal amount of encouragement, confidence, value, and self-respect. A group that has been marginalized, discouraged, and disapproved does not have a chance to access that standard of quality of life. Movements that are built on pride are an effort from within the group to build each other up and demonstrate resilience in the face of rejection. The first definition of pride carries the connotation that it does because the marginalized groups that embrace it have created for themselves the space to be proud of what others deem is shameful.

From this angle, pride appears to be harmless and even quite necessary for the health and wellness of people who are all but encouraged to live out loud. However, for a much longer time, pride has been defined more as having an excessively high sense of self-importance. By this definition, pride, vanity, arrogance, and conceit are all synonymous, because it places emphasis on how a person views and esteems self.

In American culture, pride may appear harmless, but in a relational sense, we know how damaging it actually is. It is hardest to have a thriving relationship with someone who is too proud to have productive and meaningful conversations. Those types of people do not listen to reason. They are stubborn and can be unapologetically condescending. They rarely admit wrongdoing, blame others for their problems and find it very difficult to be empathetic or see things from another person's perspective because they value their own perspective far too much. It is difficult to have a relationship with a proud person, and it is even harder to have a relationship with the Lord as long as pride exists within us.

- Pride creates justification for withholding forgiveness
- Pride causes us to weigh our logic and opinions above the Word of God.
- Pride doesn't allow us to take ownership of our own sin
- Pride creates in us a sense of being more deserving of forgiveness, than the obligation to be generous with it.

It is impossible to fully surrender as the children of God do as long as pride is perceived as a harmless necessity and the sense of self-importance that causes us to withhold forgiveness is the most detrimental of them all.

Pride goes before destruction, a haughty spirit before a fall.

Proverbs 16:18

Journal Entry:

What does 'surrender' mean to you?
In which areas of your life do you
need to lay down any pride?

Healing Through Prayer: Listening

Prayer is as much about hearing God as it is about expressing yourself to Him.

My sheep hear my voice, and I know them, and they follow me: And I give unto them eternal life; and they shall never perish, neither shall any man pluck them out of my hand.

John 10:27-28

There is a huge misconception on prayer where we tend to practice speaking to Him more than listening. Imagine if someone initiated a conversation with you, tossed you a ton of routine compliments, went on to talk about their day and their feelings, and never paused for your response. That's not a conversation at all, is it? Sometimes we hop into prayer with the right idea: giving thanks, worshipping to music, telling the Lord all the things that He has done and repenting for sin from sunup to sundown. There is a place for that, indeed, but when you are lost and hurting, that might not be something that you can do and *mean* it. What I'm saying is that prayer does not have to be just that – saying things you don't mean. The Father created a loophole for us when we don't know what to pray – it's called the Holy Spirit.

In the same way, the Spirit helps us in our weakness. We do not know what we ought to pray for, but the Spirit himself intercedes for us <u>through wordless groans</u>. And he who searches our hearts knows the mind of the Spirit, because the Spirit intercedes for God's people in accordance with the will of God. And we know that in all things God works for the good of those who love him, who have been called according to his purpose.

Romans 8:26-28

I have a challenge for you – and a challenge it will probably be. The next time you have a mind to pray, get in whatever position and space you intend to be in throughout the prayer and don't say a word for a few minutes. Don't rush or think about what you will say or how to express how you feel. Don't think about anything. Instead of thinking about how you can start or lead the conversation, silence yourself in faith knowing that God, *your Father*, will meet and sit right next to you.

Release your groans. Sway in your weakness with your mind on this promise in Romans 8:26-28. Sit and wait, knowing that He will sit with you, and that He is listening to your spirit and He knows what you need to say before you say it. Silence yourself in faith believing that if you wait for Him, He will speak to you and He will even guide you in the manner of prayer that you should pray while healing your expectations.

Before you know it, the words will come and you might be surprised that what comes out of your mouth is not even necessarily what you originally felt when you went to pray. You might find that the words that leave your lips are ones of thanksgiving and even wisdom for your own soul. You might end up praying in a completely different direction than what you felt was appropriate to pray in the headspace that you were in. In moments like those people often say, "I don't know where that came from!" but could it be that the Holy Spirit accomplished something, that you with your own intellect could not?

In this, we are essentially observing how the children of God walk after the spirit. Those who walk after the Spirit do also rely on the intercessions of the Holy Spirit. Could it be that because you were doing as the children of God do, that you were able to hear your Heavenly Father more clearly? Could it be that the direction your prayers take in those moments are then a response to what the Lord has revealed to you about yourself and your situation? If you have never experienced anything like this, try it, but understand that this is not a challenge to meditate.

Meditation is a route to train your attention and awareness, but it directs individuals to themselves, rather than to the Father. Steer clear of begrudgingly sitting with a heart posture that says *"ok, I'm here. Say something if you can."* What I am encouraging you to do is to create an intimate setting where you are allowing your spirit to perceive the voice of God – knowing that there is something in that space for you to receive if you are patient and trusting.

People tend to think that God is not speaking or that they can't hear Him because they expect Him to be in an audible voice as clear as it sounds when you're reading in your head. We are accustomed to listening with the body (ear) and the mind, but not with the spirit. So, when He does speak, they are not aware and do not know how to detect His voice. Faith allows you to stay in place to hear the voice of God so that you will actually benefit from the conversation.

Don't be discouraged if you haven't heard God's voice yet. Don't be worried if you don't know for sure what the voice of God sounds like. Apart of being a child of God comes with learning what is the Father's voice *and* what is not. It took me about six years of seeking to become even remotely aware that I was hearing the voice of the Lord and then several more before I became confident in His voice. Through reading the Word, walking with the Lord in faith, you will learn what His voice sounds like.

Journal Entry:

Write or say a prayer.

Jot words and phrases that come to you as you listen for the voice of God

Healing In Hope

And hope does not put us to shame, because God's love has been poured out into our hearts through the Holy Spirit, who has been given to us.

Romans 5:5

In that room that we called weakness, there are no mirrors. There is nothing in that room that will give you a glimpse of your future or remind you of who you are. Yet, we spend so much time in that room when we do not have the tools needed to command the space and make it one where we can find strength. With our faces to the floor and the lack of light in this room, we lose orientation and direction. Even when you look upon the walls, all you see is traumatizing memories and writings that tell a sad story. Remember, this room called weakness just as spiritual as the secret place. Therefore, all of this negativity is directly pressed upon the essence of who you are. How you view the space when you are in weakness can either yield the strength and the light of God, or it can yield more weakness and more darkness.

The eye is the lamp of the body. If your eyes are healthy, your whole body will be full of light. But if your eyes are unhealthy, your whole body will be full of darkness. If then the light within you is darkness, how great is that darkness!

Matthew 6:22-23.

In this room is where the last nail is often driven into the coffin and that is where hope is often lost. Losing hope isn't just about losing hope. Losing hope involves altogether losing yourself and losing interest or pleasure in activities that you once enjoyed. When there is overwhelming representation of darkness, it becomes difficult to envision light, even within the four walls of a church! Hope is the feeling of expectation and desire for a certain thing to happen, but we are introduced to hope outside of Christ far before we find out that there is a hope *in* Christ. That hope that we are born with leads to a ton of disappointment and it's a sad thing that most people do not receive the whole truth about how to deal with that disappointment through Jesus' Gospel of the Kingdom of God.

A part of hope involves getting back in touch with who you were *before*. If you have ever had a relationship with Jesus this might mean getting back to who you were with Jesus, but even beyond that there is significance in getting back to who you were when you felt at your best *self*. It won't begin with feeling how you felt before as much as it will be simply being able to remember what you felt before. This serves as a glimmer of light in knowing that what you experienced and felt in your weakness was not the beginning and will not be the end of your life.

The only light that can truly pierce the darkness within is the light of Jesus, but there is power in recognizing that how He designed you is a reflection of Himself. I cringe when people say that *not everything is the devil* because the I can guarantee that the enemy has investment in you feeling too defeated to manifest your calling.

How often do you participate in the things that you actually like to do? How often do you avoid people and resist temptation to do things that you drain you and do not serve you well? How would you describe yourself to someone? What is your love language? What do you need from the people around you in order to feel valued? What types of international resources do you need in order to help you be successful in your goals and pursuits?

Hope involves rediscovering yourself, valuing those things that are a part of who you are and communicating those things that make you who you are. If you can remain in touch with who you are, you can remember that there is purpose for your life. Your participation in your life is vital or else hope *is* truly lost. Not just hope for yourself but hope for those who were assigned to your life to be blessed by the gift of your existence. Those who even venture to receive Jesus and the spirit of God offer the people around them an even greater gift.

On the last and greatest day of the feast, Jesus stood up and called out in a loud voice, "If anyone is thirsty, let him come to me and drink. Whoever believes in Me, as the scripture has said: 'Streams of living water will flow from within him." He was speaking about the Spirit..."

John 7:37-39

Renovations

A new house does not build itself. It requires planning, architects, time, and strategy. Throughout this reading we have referenced the room that houses our weakness, the rooms that store our fond memories, the rooms that jail our trespassers, and the room that houses the Holy Spirit. However, in order to get to true restoration and hope, there are even more rooms that need to be entered and brought to life. What about that room that holds your career hopes? How about that room that involves having a spouse and children of your own? What ever happened to that room where you genuinely hoped and prayed for God to heal the dysfunction between your family members? Then there are those hidden rooms that are specific to your God-ordained life of which no one could possibly know. These rooms cannot be simply burned and forgotten; they need renovation.

And be not conformed to this world: but be ye transformed by the renewing of your mind, that ye may prove what is that good, and acceptable, and perfect, will of God.

Romans 12:2

The turning point is when you begin making plans to receive, understand and manifest God's will for your life by any means necessary. Your mandate to find out what is that good and acceptable, and perfect, will of God is a part of the reason you are alive. It is in the discovery and redirection that we learn God's voice and find safety in His path. Each small decision that you make to come back to yourself is about more than just that moment. Each small victory leads to the ultimate grace of being who God called you to be, but remember that in all this renovation, it requires planning, architects, time, and strategy.

This might mean that as you become more aware of the habits of your thoughts, you move in aggressive strategy to batter the thoughts that battered you. As you recognize the lulls in your day, you can make the powerful and assertive decisions to change your routine and leverage your time. This might involve planning an entire season of saying *no* to commitments and events that do not propel you into the future and the hope that you desire to achieve. You may need to design your life for seasons and spaces of intentional separation and solitude from communities and individuals that do not keep your hopes set before you. You may need to strategically post up affirmations in visible spaces and recite them over yourself even in the moments that you don't presently believe them. These practical steps taken will not make everything suddenly alright, but it is a major contributing factor to receiving the fullness of hope.

After you have done all that you can to get back to hope and renovate your house, one thing that remains is that God holds the ultimate design for your life. Even while you may still find it difficult to discern the voice of God, know that we learn His voice by getting it wrong a few times before we consistently and confidently get it right. It is an act of hope to allow the scripture to guide you in how to progress through your faith and tend to your own mental health. The God of the Bible has a lot to say about your mind. In weakness, it can be difficult to tend to the mind in a healthy or spiritual way but remember that belief in the scriptures is monumental in changing the space of weakness into that space of grace and receiving strength from a source that is outside of self. With our faces to the ground and our hope to Jesus we can ask the Lord's strength to be made perfect to show us how to renew our minds.

"...assuming that you have heard about him and were taught in him, as the truth is in Jesus, to put off your old self, which belongs to your former manner of life and is corrupt through deceitful desires, and to be renewed in the spirit of your minds, and to put on the new self, created after the likeness of God in true righteousness and holiness."

Ephesians 4:20-24

Upon this scripture we can build a prayer saying:

Lord, I am in so much pain right now, and my mind is dark and blank. I recognize that I haven't always heard or believed the truth about you but I'm learning and I trust you. Expose my deceitful desires, I give them to you — I don't want them and I don't need them. I set my mind before you to be renewed because I don't know how to renew it by myself. I have tried and it doesn't work, but I do trust You to do what I can't do. I will be who You called me to be and put on my new self as you give me strength. My way of righteousness has not served me well at all. Make me like You in true righteousness and holiness.

Amen.

According to the Word, God is only glorified to His liking when He is glorified in us, when His power is evident in our lives. The only way that His power can be manifested in our lives is if we trust that He cannot only redeem our souls from the grips of darkness but can also redeem us from our past. Redemption is our promise in the household of faith, and so naturally, there can be no testimony of redemption without depravity.

That is why faith in the Gospel and the character of God is so important. We have to believe that after all that we have experienced, do experience, and will experience, the Lord has already purposed to make something glorious out of it each and every time.

"...after you have suffered a little while, the God of all grace, who has called you to his eternal glory in Christ, will himself restore, confirm, strengthen, and establish you."

1 Peter 5:10

"The righteous person faces many troubles, but the LORD comes to the rescue each time."

Psalm 34:19

The hope we have in Jesus is beyond salvation and not limited to the churches we are a part of. In fact, the Father has desired to give us a hope *and* a future.

For I know the plans I have for you," declares the LORD, "plans to prosper you and not to harm you, plans to give you hope and a future.

Jeremiah 29:11

The Lord made this promise to the prophet Jeremiah and we hold that promise near for ourselves also because we believe it to be out of the character of God that He made this promise. The more we search the Word of God, the more promises we find and the more we test the scriptures by faith, the more we believe. We spend our lives trying to figure out why we are born and some seasons we find ourselves asking, *why don't I just die.* Nonetheless the only way to discover why we are here and how to live a life that is not limited to our experience is by going to the Father. Our hope is in the Lord because He designed us with an ultimate truth in mind.

Jesus answered, "I am the way and the truth and the life. No one comes to the Father except through me.

John 14:6

My final encouragement to you is that when you have lost your way, seek Jesus by the leading of the scriptures. The scriptures alone are not Jesus but are rather a roadmap to Him. When you have a hard time remembering the truth about yourself, believe that He has it for you; and when you have trouble believing life is worth living, seek the life that Jesus promised to us all.

As long as your hope is not in the temporary things like people, careers, and relationships, the Word of God promises that it will not put you to shame.

Seek the truth and study the scriptures, but it is your faith that will make you whole (Luke 17:19)

Journal Entry:

Take a step of faith to hope for healing in specific areas of your life.

Write down your hopes and then pair it with scripture on which you can build your prayers.

Made in the USA
Columbia, SC
11 October 2020